Just

FAQ*s

about the

HOLY SPIRIT

* Frequently Asked Questions

NELSON

Book design and composition by Robin Crosslin
Illustrations by Doug Cordes

Just the FAQs about the Holy Spirit
ISBN 0-7852-4759-9

Printed in the United States of America

1 2 3 4 5 6 7 – 07 06 05 04 03 02

FAQ #1

 Why Believe the Holy Spirit Is a Person?

 The Scriptures reveal the Holy Spirit to be a person, with all the characteristics of a living, personal being.

My brother and his wife had two children early in their marriage—a boy and a girl. On the birth of his third child, my brother quipped, "Well, I always said I wanted three children—one of each: a he, a she, and an it." His tongue was firmly in his cheek. We all got a good laugh out of it, though a couple of grandmothers didn't see the humor in it.

Much as my brother wanted "a he, a she, and an it," many people see God, in the Trinity, as a *He*, a *He*, and an *It*. I suspect the problem goes back to the King James translation of the Bible. *God* is a masculine word in the original language of the Bible, *Jesus* is a masculine word, but *Spirit* is a neuter word, a concept rather foreign to English. The word is literally "breath" or "wind," though it was also translated "spirit" or "ghost" in A.D. 1611 when the King James Bible was translated. As a result, the King James Version refers to the Holy Spirit as "it." This, plus general theological uncertainty about the Holy Spirit, has caused some to be confused as to whether He is a real person. He is, of course, and many of the more recent translations of the Bible refer to Him as "He" rather than "It," helping to dispel the impression created by the King James Version.

One key reason why we believe

> The Holy Spirit is stronger than genius.
>
> *Martin Luther*

in the "personality" of the Holy Spirit is that He has the characteristics of a person. He has intellect, emotion, and will. An example of His "intellect" is found in 1 Corinthians 2:10-11, where the Spirit is said to "know the things of God." As hard as the brightest among us struggle to know the things of God, we would have to admit that if the Holy Spirit knows the mind of God (the Father), He must have intellect. An example of His "emotions" is found in Ephesians 4:30, where we read that it is possible to grieve the Holy Spirit. You cannot grieve an impersonal force. Finally, an example of His "will" is found in 1 Corinthians 12:11, where we read that the Holy Spirit gives spiritual gifts "as He wills."

The Holy Spirit is a person not an "it."

In addition to His possessing the characteristics of personhood—intellect, emotion, and will—the Holy Spirit does things that only a person would do. The Holy Spirit teaches us, He prays for us, He performs miracles, He comforts us and guides us. These are things a *person*, not an impersonal force, would do. And though the word *spirit* is neuter in the original language of the Bible, sometimes when a pronoun is used to refer to the Holy Spirit, the pronoun *He* is used (John 16:13-14) instead of the expected *It*. This was no mistake on the part of the writers of the Bible. It was a deliberate reference to the Holy Spirit as a person.

Why I need to know who the Holy Spirit is:

1. In order to be true to the teachings of Scripture, I need to understand who the Holy Spirit is.
2. Since He is God, I need to give Him the recognition, worship, and praise that God deserves.
3. If I do not know who the Holy Spirit is, I will not enjoy a proper relationship with Him or have His full ministry in my life.

Today, those who do not believe the Holy Spirit is a person usually believe that He is merely a force emanating from God the Father. This position can be held only by mentally ripping some verses out of your Bible, pretending they aren't there. A high view of *all* of Scripture will lead a person unfailingly to the conclusion that the Holy Spirit is a person.

FAQ #2

 Why Believe the Holy Spirit Is God?

 The Scriptures reveal the Holy Spirit to be God, with all the defining characteristics of a divine being.

Saying that the Holy Spirit is a person does not say that He is God. Yet, there is ample additional evidence in Scripture to verify that He is divine. The most direct is found in Acts 5:3-4. Two converted Jews, Ananias and his wife, Sapphira, sold a piece of land they owned and brought the proceeds of the sale to give to the fledgling church in Jerusalem. They kept some of the money for themselves and gave the rest to the apostle Peter. However, they apparently lied to Peter, telling him that they were giving all the proceeds of the sale of the land to the church. Perhaps they wanted to make themselves look more spiritual. Peter learned of their deception and said, "Ananias, why has Satan filled your heart to lie to the Holy Spirit and keep back part of the price of the land for yourself? While it remained, was it not your own? And after it was sold, was it not in your own control? Why have you conceived this thing in your heart? You have not lied to men but to God." Peter declares that to lie to the Holy Spirit is to lie to God.

The Holy Spirit has divine characteristics.

In addition, the Holy Spirit has three defining characteristics of God: He is all-knowing (omniscient), all-powerful (omnipotent), and everywhere simultaneously (omnipresent). We see His omniscience in 1 Corinthians 2:10-11, "God has revealed them to us through His Spirit. For the Spirit searches all things, yes, the deep things of God. For what man knows the things of a man except the spirit of the man which is in him? Even so no one knows the things of God except the Spirit of God."

We read in the creation account in the first chapter of Genesis that the Spirit participated with God in the creation of the world, implying His omnipotence.

Finally, concerning the omnipresence of the Spirit, the writer of many of the psalms, King David, wrote, "Where can I go from Your Spirit? Or where can I flee from Your presence? If I ascend into heaven, You are there; if I make my bed in hell [Sheol, the netherworld], behold, You are there" (Psalm 139:7-8).

The Holy Spirit was responsible for the miraculous conception of Jesus, restrains sin in the world, and gives spiritual gifts to Christians. The complete evidence from Scripture leaves little doubt that the Holy Spirit is a divine person.

FAQ #3

 Why Believe the Holy Spirit Is a Member of the Trinity?

 The Scriptures reveal the Holy Spirit to be on an equal level with the Father and the Son, though distinct from them in role.

When I was growing up, I had two brothers, one two years older than I and one four years older. They were always bigger than I was and knew more than I did, so I concluded that I was short and stupid. I was neither, but no one told me that. We lived in a very small town, and one day when I was about six years old and my brothers were eight and ten, the new grocery store owner asked me my name.

"Just call me Shorty," I said in dead earnestness.

As it turned out, all three of us are now either a little over or a little under six feet tall, and each of us possesses advanced knowledge in a specialized area. It was such a revelation to me when I finally realized I was not short or stupid. There is much more equality among us now that we have grown up.

A similar point is true with the Father, Son, and Holy Spirit. An immature understanding of them might conclude that God the Father is the biggest and best, Jesus is second, and the Holy Spirit brings up the rear. A more mature understanding, however, leads us to a different conclusion. Any appearance of inequality among the Father, Son, and Holy Spirit results from differences in their roles that make one more prominent than another. The differences in role, however, do not mean inequality in personhood. A husband and a wife have different roles, but before God they are equal.

As God, the Holy Spirit is the third member of the Trinity. We deal more fully with the Trinity in another volume in this series, *Just the FAQs About God*. In historical Christian teaching, the doctrine of the Trinity states that God is one God, existing in three persons. Though the terminology gets tricky to understand, theologians and Bible teachers say God was "one God in substance but three in subsistence." Our finite minds, corrupted by the ravages of sin, cannot fully comprehend this, even though the Bible teaches it. God is three persons and yet one God. It is an "antinomy," which means, "two apparently mutually exclusive truths that must be embraced simultaneously." The truths are not really mutually exclusive, or else God would be the author of nonsense, which He isn't. But with our limited information and intellectual capacity, they appear mutually exclusive. With that understanding, God the Father, God the Son, and God the Holy Spirit are the three members of the Trinity.

We see the Father, Son, and Holy Spirit linked together

> The Father, Son, and Holy Spirit are God.

in two key New Testament passages. In 2 Corinthians 13:14, Paul writes a benediction that includes all three: "The grace of the Lord Jesus Christ, and the love of God, and the communion [fellowship] of the Holy Spirit be with you all." If Jesus and the Holy Spirit are not God, it would be presumptuous indeed to link them in the same breath with the Father.

Furthermore, in Matthew 28:19, Jesus instructs the disciples to "Go therefore and make disciples of all the nations, baptizing them in the name [not names!] of the Father and of the Son and of the Holy Spirit." James I. Packer says, "These three persons are the one God to whom Christians commit themselves" (*Concise Theology*, p. 41).

Not coincidentally, we find the members of the Trinity present at Jesus' baptism. Jesus is in the water, God the Father speaks from heaven, and the Holy Spirit descends on Him in the visible form of a dove (Mark 1:9-11).

Finally, we see the Trinitarian prayer for grace and peace from the Father, the Spirit, and Jesus Christ in Revelation 1:4-5. In the Trinitarian benediction, we see the Father mentioned first, the Son second, and the Spirit third. Yet in the Revelation passage, we see the Father first, the Spirit second, and the Son third. This capacity to alter the order of persons mentioned only reinforces their equality in the minds of the inspired writers of Scripture.

We see, then, taken in the whole, that there is ample evidence to believe the Holy Spirit is God, the third member of the Trinity.

THINKING BACK

Who is the Holy Spirit? He is the third person of the Trinity, whose role in the Godhead is less obvious to mankind than the Father and the Son but just as crucial. If we want to know God, if we want to live a vital Christian life, if we want the meaning and satisfaction of doing something deeply meaningful with our lives, if we want to understand the Scripture, if we want the ability to weather the ups and downs of life, if we want to keep a clear conscience, we need to understand who the Holy Spirit is and what His ministry is to us. We need to understand how we are to relate to Him. This subtle, behind-the-scenes Helper, Comforter, and Guide wants and needs to be a central figure in our lives. We hope that this volume will contribute to that goal. We begin by understanding that He is a person, He is God, He is the third person of the Trinity. In the name of the Father, Son, and Holy Spirit.

SPEED BUMP!

Slow down to be sure you've gotten the main points of this section.

1. **Why believe the Holy Spirit is a person?**
The Scriptures reveal the Holy Spirit to be a person, with all the characteristics of a personal being.

2. **Why believe the Holy Spirit is God?**
The Scriptures reveal the Holy Spirit to be God, with all the defining characteristics of a divine being.

3. **Why believe the Holy Spirit is a member of the Trinity?**
The Scriptures reveal the Holy Spirit to be on an equal level with the Father and the Son, though distinct from them in role.

FOR FURTHER STUDY

Scripture Passages

- **Genesis 1:2**
- **Psalm 139:7**
- **John 14:14-17, 23**
- **Acts 5:1-4**
- **1 Corinthians 2:10-11**
- **1 Corinthians 12:11, 14**
- **2 Corinthians 13:14**
- **Ephesians 4:30**

Read these passages and consider how they add to your understanding of who the Holy Spirit is.

FAQ #4

Q **What Did the Holy Spirit Do in the Old Testament?**

A **In the Old Testament, the Holy Spirit helped in creation, revealed truth to people, and empowered people to do God's will.**

To say that the Holy Spirit's job is to focus on Jesus is true of His present ministry. We see the Holy Spirit in the Old Testament, but since Jesus is not seen until the New Testament, the role of the Holy Spirit in the Old Testament could not be to focus on Jesus. So what was it?

There are three primary tasks the Holy Spirit performed in the Old Testament. He helped create the universe, He revealed the Scripture and other truth to people, and He empowered people to do things. Let's look at each of them.

Creation

It is a little confusing to talk about who is responsible for creation, because each member of the Trinity is given credit in Scripture. In Revelation 4:11 we see God sitting on a throne in heaven, surrounded by celestial beings saying to Him, "You are worthy, O Lord, to receive glory and honor and power; for You created all things, and by Your will they exist and were created." So, in this passage, creation is attributed to God the Father.

However, take a look at Colossians 1:16, which

> "My own experience is that the Bible is dull when I am dull. When I am really alive, and set upon the text with a tidal pressure of living affinities, it opens, it multiplies discoveries, and reveals depths even faster than I can note them. The worldly spirit shuts the Bible; the Spirit of God makes it a fire, flaming out all meanings and glorious truths."
>
> *Horace Bushnell (1802-1876)*

is speaking of Jesus: "For by Him all things were created that are in heaven and that are on earth, visible and invisible, whether thrones or dominions or principalities or powers. All things were created through Him and for Him."

But the Holy Spirit is not left out of the process. In Genesis 1, we read:

"In the beginning God created the heavens and the earth. And the earth was without form, and void; and darkness was on the face of the deep. And the Spirit of God was hovering over the face of the waters."

Exactly what the Spirit was doing moving over the surface of the waters is uncertain, but the context of the entire chapter is "creation," so it seems a small jump to conclude that He was involved in the creation of the world. The role of the Spirit is often seen as related to the giving of life. Job said, "The Spirit of God has made me, and the breath of the Almighty gives me life" (Job 33:4). In another passage, speaking of animal life in the sea, the psalmist wrote, "You take away their breath, they die and return to their dust. You send forth Your Spirit, they are created; and You renew the face of the earth" (Psalm 104:29-30).

God does not contradict Himself. These passages can be understood together by saying that all three members of the Trinity were involved in creation. The role of the Holy Spirit seems to have been the imparting of life, particularly when the word "spirit" and "breath" are the same word in Hebrew. When Genesis 2:7 says, "The Lord God formed man of the dust of the ground, and breathed into his nostrils the breath of life," it is not far-fetched to infer the Holy Spirit's involvement. So the Holy Spirit's role in the Old Testament included creation.

Revelation

A second activity of the Holy Spirit in the Old Testament was revealing God's truth to humanity. God's chief human instrument for giving His message to humanity was the prophet. These were usually men who ran the gamut of society. Some were uneducated, counter-

The Holy Spirit's job is to draw light on Jesus.

culture, reclusive people, while others were refined, sophisticated, highly educated, and highly placed in society. Yet they all had one thing in common. God had chosen them to be instruments of His direct revelation that they, in turn, were responsible to communicate to God's chosen audience. The apostle Peter wrote: "No prophecy was ever made by an act of human will, but men moved by the Holy Spirit spoke from God" (2 Peter 1:21, NASB). In 2 Samuel 23:1-2, King David identifies himself as the writer of Psalms, and says, "The Spirit of the Lord spoke by me, and His word was on my tongue." So we see that the Holy Spirit was the agent who revealed God's truth to humanity through prophets and through the Scriptures.

The Holy Spirit empowered people to do the will of God.

Power

Finally, the Holy Spirit empowered people to do the will of God. When the leadership of the Israelites was being transferred from Moses to his protégé, Joshua, the Lord said to Moses, "Take Joshua the son of Nun with you, a man in whom is the Spirit, and lay your hand on him; set him before Eleazar the priest and before all the congrega-

Why I need to know what the Holy Spirit does:

1. To have a proper appreciation for the Holy Spirit and an adequate capacity to worship Him.
2. To avoid falling into error concerning the ministry of the Holy Spirit.
3. To make sure I do not miss out on the Holy Spirit's ministry in my life.

tion, and inaugurate him in their sight. And you shall give some of your authority to him, that all the congregation of the children of Israel may be obedient" (Numbers 27:18-20).

The Holy Spirit even came upon seemingly undeserving people to accomplish God's will. Samson, for example, was one of the least deserving people in the Bible for God to work through in a mighty way, and yet He did. The Philistines, the enemies and oppressors of Israel during Samson's day, ambushed the powerful Samson, thinking they had subdued him with ropes. But "the Spirit of the Lord came mightily upon [Samson]; and the ropes that were on his arms became like flax that is burned with fire, and his bonds broke loose from his hands. He found a fresh jawbone of a donkey, reached out his hand and took it, and killed a thousand men with it" (Judges 15:14-15). The Holy Spirit also came upon King Saul of Israel, and King David, and others to empower them to do the will of God.

Whether prophet, priest, or king, shepherd, judge, or soldier, we see the Holy Spirit coming upon people in the Old Testament to empower them to accomplish the will of God.

FAQ #5

Q

What Did the Holy Spirit Do in the New Testament?

A

In the New Testament, the Holy Spirit empowered the ministry of Jesus and His church.

There are a lot of great stories: Cinderella, Sleeping Beauty, Snow White and the Seven Dwarfs. Beauty and the Beast is a great story, though I am referring to the original story, not the Disney animated version familiar to most people. The original story is much better. On a loftier scale, you could add *A Tale of Two Cities*, *Jane Eyre*, and *Les Miserables*. But the greatest story of all time, even for people who do not believe it to be true, is the story of the birth, life, death, and resurrection of Jesus. All the other great stories are shadows and echoes by comparison. The fact that the story of Jesus is true lifts it out of the profound into its own earthshaking category, and it cannot be told apart from the Holy Spirit.

Jesus' Birth

In Luke 1:26, the angel Gabriel visited a young Jewish maiden named Mary. Was it in the middle of the night? Was she alone? Was she frightened? He told her she would be having a child. Did he speak to her audibly, or did the thoughts merely enter her mind? Was he visible in any way? Was it a dream or vision? Mary's obvious question was, "How can this be, since I do not know a man?" Gabriel spoke some of the most amazing words ever heard by the human ear: "The Holy Spirit will come upon you, and the power of the Highest will overshadow you; therefore, also, that Holy One who is to be born will be called the Son of God."

The Holy Spirit was active in and through the life of Jesus.

What an amazing and touching scene! An unknown Jewish maiden becomes the earthly mother of Jesus of Nazareth by the miraculous conception of the Holy Spirit. From this astonishing beginning, to the bittersweet end, the Holy Spirit was active in and through the life of Jesus.

Jesus' Baptism

When Jesus was baptized, we see the Holy Spirit again, descending on Jesus in the form of a dove (Luke 4:18). This confirmed, along with the voice of God the Father speaking from heaven, the special nature of Jesus' life and empowered Him for ministry. The apostle Peter acknowledges this in Acts 10:38 when he said, "You know…how God anointed Jesus of Nazareth with the Holy Spirit and with power, who went about doing good and healing all who were oppressed by the devil, for God was with Him."

Jesus' Life and Ministry

Immediately after Jesus was baptized, He was led by the Spirit out into the wilderness where He was tempted by Satan (Matthew 4:1-11). John 3:34 says, "For He whom God has sent speaks the words of God;

for He gives the Spirit without measure" (NASB). Apparently, God gave the Holy Spirit to Jesus, and that is what enabled Jesus to speak the words of God. Jesus was empowered by the Holy Spirit to do miracles. In Matthew 12:28, we read, "If I (Jesus) cast out demons by the Spirit of God, surely the kingdom of God has come upon you." Jesus' ability to cast out demons was a result of the power of the Holy Spirit within Him.

In summary, we see that Jesus was led by the Spirit, filled with the Spirit, enabled to preach, teach, and exhort by the Spirit, and empowered to do miracles by the Holy Spirit.

Jesus' Death, Burial, and Resurrection

At the end of Jesus' life, the Holy Spirit continued to minister to Him. If Hebrews 9:14 refers to the Holy Spirit, and not Christ's own spirit as some believe, then Jesus offered Himself as a sacrifice through the Holy Spirit: "How much more shall the blood of Christ, who through the eternal Spirit offered Himself without spot to God, cleanse your conscience from dead works to serve the living God?"

Romans 1:4 may refer to the Spirit's involvement in the resurrection of Jesus: "[Jesus] was declared the Son of God with power by the resurrection from the dead, according to the spirit of holiness" (NASB). And finally, Jesus gave commandments to the apostles (and through them to us) by the Holy Spirit: "[Jesus] was taken up, after He through the Holy Spirit had given commandments to the apostles whom He had chosen" (Acts 1:2). So we see, from beginning to end, the Holy Spirit was involved in the life of Jesus of Nazareth.

Revelation

Just as the Holy Spirit revealed God's truth to people in the Old Testament, so He did in the New Testament. He gave people visions and dreams (Acts 10:1-20) and revealed prophecies and Scripture as He guided the authors of the New Testament (2 Peter 1:21; 3:15-16; 2 Timothy 3:16-17).

The Church

Finally, the Holy Spirit gave birth to the church in the New Testament. In the Old Testament, God chose the nation of Israel to receive His message of salvation and to carry that message to the world

(Psalm 67). In the New Testament, God chose the church for that lofty task. It is easy to identify Israel. Israel is all the people who were descendants of Abraham, plus those who converted to Judaism. It is a little harder to identify the church. The church is the totality of all believers in Jesus. When a person becomes a Christian, he automatically becomes a member of the church. It is to the church that God has given the New Testament message of salvation and, it is by the power of the Holy Spirit that the church takes that message to the ends of the earth (Acts 1:8).

FAQ #6

 What Does the Holy Spirit Do Today?

 Today, the Holy Spirit helps Christians know, be, and do what God wants.

After I graduated from seminary, I received a position teaching in a Christian college in Arizona. My wife and I quit our jobs and moved to Arizona in August—not a good time to move. (Someone once said there are three reasons not to live in Arizona: June, July, and August!) School started the first of September. We spent our meager reserves of cash getting moved, paying the deposits on the apartment, utilities, and so forth. And, since we got paid once a month, we were not to receive our first paycheck until the last of September. The bottom line was, we ran out of money. When you run out of money, you also run out of food. We had about two weeks to go before our first paycheck. There was no money in the bank and only about six eggs in the house. We were invited to the academic dean's house for dinner one night, and I must have eaten an unusual amount of food, because somehow the subject turned to how we were making it financially. Since the dean and his wife were asking out of compassion and very directly, we told them. They opened their well-stocked freezer and gave us enough food to last us until our first paycheck. It was slightly humiliating, but deeply appreciated. They helped us when we really needed it.

There have been many times when Margie and I have received help when we really needed it. Sometimes people have helped us load our truck when we were moving. People have let us live with them during periods of transition. Others have surrounded us with love and compassion during times of grave illness. Others have helped us capitalize on opportunities by putting in a good word for us. Friends have come close to us when we were lonely. When we look back over our lives, we see an endless stream of people who helped us overcome difficulties or just made life easier.

The Holy Spirit helps those who are Christians.

You are doing something godly when you help others, because that is the primary ministry of God the Holy Spirit to us—to help us. Five times in the Gospel of John the Holy Spirit is called our Helper. If we were to summarize what the Holy Spirit does today, we would say that He helps those who are Christians.

When we are down, He helps us up. When we need a shove, He gets us moving in the right direction. When we need wisdom, He opens our mind to God's word. He helps us witness to Jesus both by opening the door of opportunity and by giving us the words to share. The Holy Spirit helps believers in many ways, as the rest of the book will demonstrate.

FAQ #7

 What Will the Holy Spirit Do in the Future?

 In the future, the Holy Spirit will help bring history to an end and usher in eternity.

We don't know as much about the future as we wish we did. We would like to know how things are going to unfold for us personally, when the end of the world will come, and what life will be like after that. We also do not know as much about the ministry of the Holy

Spirit in the future as we wish we did. Most of what is said about the Spirit's ministry in the future is veiled in mystery, and there are usually at least two responsible opinions as to what the Scripture means in these instances.

Some believe that 2 Thessalonians 2:7 teaches that there will be a day when the Holy Spirit, who restrains sin in the world, will be removed from the earth as a pervasive presence restraining sin, and that a conflagration of sin will erupt like an unattended forest fire. Others believe that when Joel 2 was quoted in Acts 2:17-21 it was not a complete fulfillment of Joel's prophecy, so the prophecy will be finally fulfilled at some time in the future. If that is the case, the Spirit will be involved in some pretty dramatic events in the future, such as the sun turning to darkness and the moon turning to blood, and visions and dreams being rather widespread.

Also, in comparing Zechariah 4:1-6 with Revelation 11:3-4, we see the Holy Spirit being involved in some rather apocalyptic events at some time in the future. How literally these events are to be interpreted and when they might happen is not a matter of complete agreement in the Christian community, so the Spirit's role here is a matter of educated speculation. But whatever these passages mean, we see the Spirit involved and His power revealed to an awesome extent.

THINKING BACK

To conclude this overview section, I want to focus on the whole subject of helping others. There is an old poem which reads,

Let me live in my house by the side of the road
  Where the race of men go by—
They are good, they are bad, they are weak, they are strong.
  Wise, foolish—so am I.
Then why should I sit in the scorner's seat

> **Or hurl the cynic's ban?**
> **Let me live in my house by the side of the road**
> **And be a friend to man.**
> **(Sam Walter Foss, "The House by the Side of the Road,"**
> **quoted by William Bennett, *The Book of Virtues*,**
> **pp. 305-306)**

It sounds foreign to us today. It is so risky to help people. If you pick up a hitchhiker, he may rob you and steal your car. If you open your door to a stranger on a stormy night, he may assault you. If you give money to someone who seems to need it, he may have lied to you and spend the money on drugs or alcohol.

When you help others, you are imitating what God does for us.

Today, therefore, we might write,

> **Let me live in my house on the cul-de-sac**
> **where no one ever drives by.**
> **Men are bad, they are weak, they will lie and will steal.**
> **Be a victim? No, not I.**
> **Let them ply their wicked trade of life**
> **On less suspecting souls.**
> **Let me live in my house on the cul-de-sac**
> **Where trouble never tolls.**

It is certainly true that life is more complicated than it used to be. It is harder to help people than it used to be, but that doesn't mean we should stop trying. Certainly it may be unwise to put ourselves or our families in danger, but there are a thousand "safe" ways we can help people if we will.

Churches often get calls from people needing money or help of some kind, and many times you don't know if the calls are legitimate. I had to develop a policy of almost never giving anyone money, because we discovered that panhandlers who wanted the money for alcohol soon learned who the "soft touches" were. It was like getting your name on some bad mailing list. You soon had more sob stories than you knew how to handle. We would buy people groceries, or pay their rent or electric bill, but almost never give them money.

There were times when the appeals for help were obviously legitimate and times when they obviously weren't. But there were times when you just didn't know. In those times, as a church, we decided God would rather have us waste some of His money on people who didn't deserve it than fail to give it to someone who really needed it.

Yes, it is hard to help people these days. But if we have a heart that lives "by the side of the road" instead of on the cul-de-sac, we will find ways to help that are safe and appropriate. And when you help others, you are imitating what God does for us every day.

SPEED BUMP!

Slow down to be sure you've gotten the main points of this section.

1. **What did the Holy Spirit do in the Old Testament?**
In the Old Testament, the Holy Spirit helped in creation, revealed truth to people, and empowered people to do God's will.

2. **What did the Holy Spirit do in the New Testament?**
In the New Testament, the Holy Spirit empowered the ministry of Jesus and His church.

3. **What does the Holy Spirit do today?**
Today, the Holy Spirit helps Christians know, be, and do what God wants.

4. **What will the Holy Spirit do in the future?**
In the future, the Holy Spirit will help bring history to an end and usher in eternity.

FOR FURTHER STUDY

Scripture Passages

- Genesis 1
- Judges 15:14-15
- 2 Samuel 23:1-2
- Psalm 67
- Matthew 4:1-11

- Luke 1:35
- Luke 4:18
- Acts 2:17-21
- Acts 10:38
- Romans 1:4

FAQ #8

 What Is Conviction?

 Conviction is the ministry of the Holy Spirit in which He causes us to recognize our sin and prompts us to turn from it.

Central Passage: **John 16:8, When He [the Holy Spirit] has come, He will convict the world of sin, and of righteousness, and of judgment.**

"Through his death on the cross Jesus Christ not only readjusts a man in conscience and heart to God, he does something grander; he imparts to him the power to do all God wants, he presences him with divinity, the Holy Spirit, so that he is garrisoned from within, and enabled to live without blame before God."

Oswald Chambers (1874-1917)

Conviction was what I experienced during my moral collapse in my first year in college—the gut-wrenching realization that I was trapped in a lifestyle that I didn't want but didn't have the strength to pull myself out of. I understood very well where the phrase "guilty as sin" came from. I felt guilty as sin, because I was. I believed I was sinning and ought to stop. That is the beginning point for salvation. Even if someone understands all about salvation, he will make no attempt to receive it unless he first comes to recognize that he is a sinner and wants to do something about it. When you are discussing salvation with someone and he has no conviction of sin, no sense of his need for Christ, you will get nowhere. There were times in my life when people talked to me about salvation, and I told them to mind their own business. I had no conviction of sin. I had no sense of separation from God and a need to be reconciled to Him.

In 2 Corinthians 4:3-4, we read, "If our gospel is veiled, it is veiled to those who are

Why I need to know the role of the Holy Spirit in my salvation:

1. I need to understand that I cannot come to Christ except as He is working in my life. The same is true about others to whom I may be ministering.

2. If I don't understand this, it might put me on a guilt trip, thinking that if I had done more, someone else might have become a Christian. If I don't understand that I am merely a conveyer of information—that salvation is between a person and God—I may take up a burden that is simply too great for me to carry.

3. If I don't understand the Holy Spirit's role in my salvation, I will not appreciate completely what He has done for me, and it will limit my joy and my capacity to worship God.

perishing, whose minds the god of this age [Satan] has blinded, who do not believe, lest the light of the gospel of the glory of Christ, who is the image of God, should shine on them." As long as someone is blinded by Satan, he will feel no conviction of sin. That is why, when we talk or preach or write to others about Christ, our first line of offense is prayer. Our clever arguments will never win anyone to Christ. Our powers of persuasion, our magnetic personality, our depth of relationship are all as powerless as a floodlight on a forest fire to convince anyone of a need for Christ. Only if the person is convicted of sin, recognizes that sin has separated him from God, and desires to be reconciled to God will that one accept the gospel of Christ.

Without the Spirit, our witness gets nowhere.

As I said, no one can bring another person to Christ. Only God can bring someone to Christ, and conviction of sin is the first step. This is what was behind Jesus' statement in John 6:44, "No one can come to Me unless the Father who sent Me draws him; and I will raise him up at the last day." The Father draws us through the Holy Spirit.

Therefore, in sharing our faith we must recognize that our task is to pray and rely on God entirely for His work in the life of the individual with whom we are dealing. We are responsible to share Christ with others, but we cannot determine whether or not that person will come to Christ. That is between the person and Christ.

There are those who have come to Christ on the prompting of the slightest off-the-cuff remark, and there are those who have been raised in godly Christian homes, hearing the truth and seeing it lived all their lives, who never come to Christ. Salvation is a work of God, not a work of man. Proclamation is our work. We give the Good News and we pray. God does everything else.

FAQ #9

 What Is Regeneration?

 Regeneration is the ministry of the Holy Spirit in which He causes us to be born again, spiritually resulting in eternal life.

Central Passage: **Titus 3:5 (NASB), He saved us, not on the basis of deeds which we have done in righteousness, but according to His mercy, by the washing of regeneration and renewing by the Holy Spirit.**

Phoenix was the Greek name for the mythological bird that was sacred to the sun-god in ancient Egypt. An eaglelike bird with red and gold plumage (as Herodotus described it), the phoenix lived in Arabia and had a five hundred-year life span. At the end of that period the bird built its own funeral pyre, on which it was consumed to ashes. Out of the ashes a new phoenix arose. The cycle was repeated every five hundred years.

In a sense, that is what happens to the Christian. Mankind has self-destructed, burning himself to ashes on his own funeral pyre of sin. "But God, who is rich in mercy, because of His great love with which He loved us, even when we were dead in trespasses, made us alive together with Christ" (Ephesians 2:4-5). Out of the ashes, we rise to new life in Christ. The dramatic story of the phoenix became popular with some medieval Christian writers as a symbol of death and resurrection.

Eternal life follows death to sin.

"We were dead in our trespasses and sins," Paul wrote. In what sense were we dead? Obviously we were not dead physically. We were dead spiritually, which means separated from God. It is like a husband and wife who no longer love each other. Hostility and rejection lie at the core of their relationship. They do not talk to each other. They no longer live in the same house. Their relationship, we say, is dead. It means more than that to be dead in our trespasses and sins before God, but at least that example gives us a glimpse of the meaning. It does not mean that we have ceased living, spiritually. It means we are separated, cut off, alienated from God.

Our spirit has been contaminated with sin, and God cannot tolerate the presence of sin. Therefore, apart from His amazing love for us, He cannot tolerate us. There is only one hope. Our old self, con- taminated with sin, must die. That is what Paul meant when he said, "I have been crucified with Christ" (Galatians 2:20). Spiritually, in a way we do not fully understand, we are placed in Christ, and the crucifixion that He experienced, we experi- ence. The death that He died, we die. That gets rid of the sin. Then, by the ministry of the Holy Spirit, we are born again, this time to new life. This time, we are without sin in our inner man (Romans 7:15—8:1).

New birth makes us righteous before God.

We still sin, but somehow, again in ways that I am not sure we fully understand, the sin is not attributed to our spirit, our inner man; it is assigned to our flesh. There is nothing else that needs to happen to our spirit before it can go to heaven. Paul wrote in Ephesians 4:24 (NASB), "Put on the new self which, in the likeness of God has been created in righteousness and holiness of the truth."

What an astonishing statement. Our new self, after we have been born again, is in the likeness of God, in righteousness and holiness.

Of course, we all know that we sin, but Paul steadfastly refuses to attribute the sin to the new self. He goes out of his way to place it in what he calls "the flesh" (NASB). "If I am doing the very thing I do not wish, I am no longer the one doing it, but sin which dwells in me" (Romans 7:20 NASB).

He completes this thought in Romans 8:23: "We ourselves groan within ourselves, eagerly waiting for the adoption, the redemption of our body." His point here is that our complete redemption will not occur until we die and get a new body, uncontaminated by sin. We could say that we are redeemed in stages. One stage is our spiritual redemption when we are born again. Another stage is our progressive spiritual growth while on earth. A third stage is our physical redemption, when we receive new bodies, either when we die or when Jesus comes again, whichever comes first.

Regeneration is that act of the Holy Spirit by which He causes us to be born again spiritually, at the moment we place our faith in Christ.

With this as background, read the condensed account from John 3 where Jesus talks to Nicodemus, a religious leader of the Jews, about his need to be born again, and see if it doesn't make sense to you:

Now there was a man of the Pharisees, named Nicodemus, a ruler of the Jews; this man came to Him by night, and said to Him, "Rabbi, we know that You have come from God as a teacher; for no one can do these signs that You do unless God is with him." Jesus answered and said to him, "Truly, truly, I say to you, unless one is born again, he cannot see the kingdom of God." Nicodemus said to Him, "How can a man be born when he is old? He cannot enter a second time into his mother's womb and be born, can he?" Jesus answered, "Truly, truly, I say to you, unless one is born of…the Spirit, he cannot enter into the kingdom of God…Do not marvel that I said to you, 'You must be born again.'…As Moses lifted up the serpent in the wilderness, even so must the Son of Man be lifted up, that whoever believes may in Him have eternal life. For God so loved the world, that He gave His only begotten Son, that whoever believes in Him should not perish, but have eternal life. (NASB)

One of the ministries that the Holy Spirit has in our salvation is causing us to be born again spiritually, resulting in eternal life.

FAQ #10

 What Is Indwelling?

 Indwelling is the ministry of the Holy Spirit coming to live in the body of each Christian.

Central Passage: 1 Corinthians 6:19-20, Do you not know that your body is the temple of the Holy Spirit who is in you, whom you have from God, and you are not your own? For you were bought at a price; therefore glorify God in your body.

Misunderstanding the concept of "indwelling" was where I got into trouble the night I became a Christian. As I said, I had the idea that there was a Max-shaped spirit sitting beside me that I had to get to merge with my shape, like focusing a camera or a pair of binoculars. The concept of indwelling is such a mystery that probably none of us understands specifically what happens in the process. But indwelt we are if we give our lives over to following Christ. The Scripture makes it clear that the Holy Spirit is in us, and based on that fact, we should glorify God in our bodies.

Every believer is permanently indwelt. The Holy Spirit does not move in and move out like an unstable tenant. Nor does He move in and out depending on whether he likes the condition of the "temple" He is in. Indwelling is permanent. Once He comes to take up residence in you, He stays forever. Jesus made that plain when he said, "I will pray the Father, and He will give you another Helper, that He may abide with you forever-the Spirit of truth, whom the world cannot receive, because it neither sees Him nor knows Him; but you know Him, for He dwells with you and will be in you" (John 14:16-17).

We sometimes fear that if we sin the Holy Spirit will leave us. While there are plenty of things to dread if we willfully and flagrantly persist in sin (Hebrews 12:5-11), losing the Holy Spirit is not one of them. As we just saw, Jesus sent the Helper "that He may abide with you forever."

If anyone was going to lose the Holy Spirit, it would have been some of the Christians in the ancient church in Corinth. One church member was committing adultery with his stepmother (1 Corinthians 5:5)! Others were suing the socks off each other (1 Corinthians 6)! Others apparently were visiting prostitutes (1 Corinthians 6:15). Paul says of them, "You are still not spiritual, because there is jealousy and quarreling among you, and this shows that you are not spiritual. You are acting like people of the world" (1 Corinthians 3:3, New Century Version). And so they were—somewhat like the church in America! Yet, in spite of this, Paul tells these people that the indwelling of the Spirit is permanent. It is precisely because the Holy Spirit is indwelling them that Paul urges them not to defile their bodies with sexual immorality (Romans 6:18-20).

Indwelling is once and for always.

There are two ways a Christian can know that he is indwelt by the Holy Spirit. First, simply take the Scripture at face value. If you have believed in and received Christ as your personal savior, you have the Spirit. In fact, Romans 8:9 makes it clear that if you don't have the Spirit you are not saved, while if you do have the Spirit, you are. The second way is to look for the evidence of His work in your life. When I became a Christian, I was not sure I was, because I couldn't keep the Holy Spirit's spiritual outline in focus with my physical outline. But the next day, I went to work at my summer construction job, and it really bothered me that everyone was swearing. No matter that the day before I was leading the uncouth chorus, today I wanted everybody to shut up. Why did they have to take Jesus' name in vain? I wondered. I also quit drinking, smoking, and hanging out with the wrong kind of people. On the other side of things, I found myself reading my Bible, especially the Gospel of John, over and over again. I started going to church, and developed a desire to talk to other Christians about spiritual things. A desire to be more loving, less prideful, and more patient sprang up deep within me. Not everyone's experience will be the same as mine, but "change" is a sign of the indwelling Spirit of God.

Because the Spirit indwells us, we are never alone. Prisoners in concentration camps or prisoner of war camps testify that the presence of God kept them going during the grueling hours, days, and even years of solitude, because they knew they were not really alone.

FAQ #11

 What Is Baptism?

 Baptism of the Holy Spirit is the ministry of the Spirit incorporating the Christian into the body of Christ.

Central Passage: **Romans 6:3-5 (NASB), Or do you not know that all of us who have been baptized into Christ Jesus have been baptized into His death? Therefore we have been buried with Him through baptism into death, in order that as Christ was raised from the dead through the glory of the Father, so we too might walk in newness of life. For if we have become united with Him in the likeness of His death, certainly we shall be also in the likeness of His resurrection.**

Christians agree widely concerning the Holy Spirit's work in our salvation, and that body of agreement provides a common perspective on much of the Christian life. The definition and purpose of the baptism of the Holy Spirit, however, is one of the areas that is widely debated. While we look at varying perspectives in this section, we emphasize that, while there may be differences of understanding on this issue among Christians, there is fundamental agreement on the basics of the Christian faith that we share, and we therefore survey the differences with a spirit of mutual respect.

The Classic Evangelical View

The mainstream evangelical position, which reflects my own view, understands baptism of the Holy Spirit to be that work of the Holy Spirit in which He places each believer into the body of Christ at the moment of conversion. First Corinthians 12:13 says, "For by one Spirit we were all baptized into one body—whether Jews or Greeks, whether slaves or free—and have all been made to drink into one Spirit."

From the central passage in Romans 6, from Acts 1:4-5, and from this Corinthian passage, evangelicals draw several observations:

1. All believers are baptized by the Spirit.

2. Spirit baptism happens at the moment of conversion.

3. Apparently each believer is baptized only once.

4. It makes all believers members of the body of Christ.

The Body of Christ: The body of Christ is a figure of speech, meaning "the totality of all believers in Jesus." It is the totality of all Christians who have ever lived, past, present, and future. It is synonymous in the Bible with the "church." This "universal church" is the same as the body of Christ. Local churches are local, visible, organized groups of people who may or may not be members of the universal church, the body of Christ. If a person is not a Christian, he may attend a local church, even be a member of the local church. But because he is not a Christian, he is not a member of the universal church, the body of Christ. You may have heard the old saying that going to local church doesn't make a person a Christian any more than going to a garage makes someone a car. That is the point here.

Baptize: To baptize means, primarily, "to dip." It is used in the Bible of people taking baths, of dying a garment, or of drawing water by dipping a cup into the water.

To be baptized by the Holy Spirit, according to this perspective, means to be placed, or incorporated spiritually into the body of Christ. It is as if the body of Christ were an ocean of people, and we, as individuals, are placed into it. "We have been buried with Him through *baptism* into death," Paul writes in Romans 6:3 (NASB, italics added). Verse 5 goes on to mention that "if we have become *united* with Him in the likeness of His death, certainly we shall be also in the likeness of His resurrection (NASB, italics added)." The inference can be drawn, then, that being baptized into Christ means "being united with Him," as well as with all other believers in the body of Christ.

Some evangelicals apply the term baptism to one's first experience of being filled with the Spirit. However, many evangelicals understand that while speaking in tongues and other miraculous events occurred in the New Testament, they were not a manifestation of the baptism of the Holy Spirit, but rather a result of the miraculous filling of the Holy Spirit (Acts 2:4). The filling of the Holy Spirit will be discussed in a later chapter. The baptism of the Spirit, as we said, simply places one into the spiritual body of Christ.

Billy Graham articulated this view of Spirit baptism in his book, *The Holy Spirit*, when he wrote:

Many years ago when I was attending a small Bible school in Florida, I visited what was called a "brush arbor revival meeting." The speaker was an old fashioned Southern revival preacher. The little place seated about two hundred people and was filled. The speaker made up in thunder what he lacked in logic, and the people loved it.

"Have you been baptized with the Holy Spirit?"

Apparently he knew a great many in the audience because he would point to someone and ask, "Brother, have you been baptized with the Spirit?" And the man would answer, "Yes, bless God."

"Young man," he said, spotting me, "have you been baptized with the Holy Spirit?" "Yes, sir," I replied.

"When were you baptized with the Holy Spirit?" he asked. He had not questioned the others on this.

"The moment I received Jesus Christ as my Savior," I replied. He looked at me with a puzzled expression, but before going to the next person he said, "That couldn't be."

But it could! It was.

I do not doubt the sincerity of this preacher. However, in my own study of the Scriptures through the years I have become convinced that there is only one baptism with the Holy

Spirit in the life of every believer, and that takes place at the
moment of conversion (pp. 89-90).

The Pentecostal/Charismatic View

Perhaps Graham had attended a Pentecostal revival. In the
Pentecostal and charismatic view, "baptism in the Holy Spirit" differs
from the mainstream evangelical view both in its definition and its purpose. In this view, Jesus baptizes already converted believers with the
Holy Spirit in order to empower them to live and minister as Jesus did.

They believe this for two key reasons: the example of Jesus and
the example of the early church in Acts. Regarding Jesus, when He was
baptized by John the Baptist, the Holy Spirit descended upon Him,
and He was described as "being filled with the Holy Spirit" when He
entered His forty days of temptation (Luke 3:22; 4:1). After His temptation, Jesus entered public ministry "in the power of the Spirit" and
with the Spirit's anointing (Luke 4:14, 18-19).

This tradition emphasizes that Jesus is to be seen not only as
unique, but also as an example to be followed. As God, as Messiah, as
Savior, as the Son of God, Jesus is unique and unrepeatable. But as one
whose ministry is empowered by the Holy Spirit, Jesus is a prototype
for all believers who may and can be similarly empowered by the Holy
Spirit to continue Jesus' earthly ministry now that He is gone.

The Book of Acts begins by strongly connecting the ministry
of Jesus while He was on earth with His ongoing ministry
through the early church (Acts 1:1). While the Gospel
of Luke, the companion to Acts, recorded what
"Jesus began to do and teach," Acts
records what Jesus continued to do
through the divine power of
the Holy Spirit and Jesus' followers. Just as Jesus Himself was
empowered by the Holy Spirit, so believers are to be also. The "Promise of the Father"
is given when Jesus baptizes believers with (or by
or in) the Holy Spirit, Who empowers believers to witness effectively to Jesus throughout the world (Acts 1:4-8).

The Pentecostal/charismatic view of Spirit baptism links Jesus'
ministry with the similar experiences of his followers in the Book of Acts

Evangelicals
believe all Christians are
baptized by the
Holy Spirit.

when the Spirit came upon them (2:1-4; 4:31; 8:14-17; 11:12-17; 19:1-6). Baptism in the Holy Spirit is seen to be distinct from conversion (although nothing in principle prevents Spirit baptism at conversion) and distinct from the purpose of incorporating a believer into Christ's body. Spirit baptism instead introduces the Christian to the fullness of the Christian life that God intended. It also empowers the believer for effective ministry, complete with the same kinds of supernatural works that characterize His ministry.

Pentecostals see baptism in the Spirit as a second work of grace.

Drawing upon the examples in the Book of Acts of the Spirit's coming upon and filling believers, Pentecostals and charismatics understand that when believers are baptized in the Spirit, they know it: The coming of the Spirit is experienced, as the various descriptions of Acts indicate, usually including speaking in tongues. Some Pentecostals and charismatics do not insist that Spirit baptism is always accompanied by speaking in tongues, but do maintain that some sort of Spirit-inspired speech signifies the Spirit's coming and giving the power to witness to Christ effectively.

Traditional Wesleyan teaching also emphasizes that the baptism of the Holy Spirit is distinct from conversion and leads to fullness of Christian life and effective service. Generally, however, Wesleyan believers do not embrace other Pentecostal and charismatic practices, such as speaking in tongues.

While the Pentecostal/charismatic tradition sees the baptism of the Holy Spirit as distinct from conversion (unlike the classic evangelical view that sees it as part of and simultaneous with conversion), it is seen as part of an essential process, the whole of which includes "conversion + water baptism + Spirit baptism" (see Acts 2:38). That is, God wants each Christian to experience conversion, water baptism, and Spirit baptism as entry into the fullness of Christian life and ministry.

Conversion is essential, of course, because that is the moment at which a person becomes a Christian. Water baptism is important because it is commanded by our Lord (Matthew 28:19-20). Spirit baptism is important because it is essential to empower the Christian for fullness of the Christian life and full effectiveness in ministry.

Other issues related closely to the Pentecostal/charismatic tradition's understanding of the Holy Spirit baptism, such as the role of signs and wonders and spiritual gifts in contemporary biblical Christianity, will be addressed elsewhere in the book.

Summary

All evangelical Christians, including those in the Pentecostal/charismatic tradition who differ on their understanding of "baptism of the Holy Spirit," agree that the Holy Spirit incorporates all believers into the body of Christ at the point of their conversion and new birth. All evangelical Christians also believe that miraculous things happened in the Book of Acts surrounding the fillings and baptisms of the Holy Spirit. The two primary differences in understanding between the two traditions include the definition of Spirit baptism (and whether or not the miraculous events in Acts were a result of that baptism or of a special Spirit filling) and whether the miracles accompanying the lives of Jesus and His disciples are intended to be duplicated in the ministry of the church in all times.

FAQ #12

 What Is Sealing?

 Sealing of the Holy Spirit is the ministry of the Spirit marking us as God's own possession and guaranteeing our salvation.

Central Passage: **Ephesians 1:13-14 (NASB), In [Christ], you also, after listening to the message of truth, the gospel of your salvation—having also believed, you were sealed in Him with the Holy Spirit of promise, who is given as a pledge of our inheritance.**

The sealing of the Holy Spirit marks us as God's own possession. The Holy Spirit within us is that mark. One of the best days of my life came when I was invited to participate with a rancher in branding the yearling calves. We rode out onto the range and drove the cattle with new calves to a holding pen. There we caught each calf and burned a brand into its hip. The brand is unique, registered to that rancher. No other rancher can have the same brand. The brand says, "This calf belongs to John Q. Rancher," and no one can dispute it. The Holy Spirit is God's brand on us.

Not only does the seal signify ownership, it also signifies authority. One of my favorite stories picturing the power and signifi- cance of a seal is that of an emissary that Alexander the Great once sent to Egypt. This representative of the most pow- erful man on earth at the time traveled to Egypt without weapons or military escort. He carried only the seal of Alexander, possibly a signet ring bearing Alexander's official seal.

Sealing **signifies ownership and authority.**

The emissary met with the king of Egypt, who stood with his army behind him, and communicated to him that Alexander wanted him to cease hostilities against Alexander's interests. The king of Egypt, wishing to save face, said that he would consider Alexander's request and let him know later what his response would be.

At that, the emissary drew a circle in the dirt around the king of Egypt and said, "Do not leave the circle without informing me of your response."

Think of that! The king of Egypt was standing there in full mili- tary array, with his army instantly ready to obey his commands. The emissary was unarmed. Yet the king dared not harm or defy the emis- sary without defying Alexander. Whatever he did to the emissary, he did to Alexander. Realizing that he was facing, by extension, Alexander himself, after a long, tense moment he said, "Tell Alexander he has his request," and stepped out of the circle.

That is the power of a seal. It carries the full weight of the one who owns it. We have God's seal, the Holy Spirit, which carries the full weight of God the Father behind it (2 Corinthians 1:22). The seal signifies that we are God's possession, that we have God's authority behind us, and it guarantees our security.

This seal, Paul says in Ephesians 1:13-14, is also a pledge, a down payment. The presence of the Holy Spirit indwelling us guarantees the final purchase price when our bodies are redeemed in heaven.

The trucking industry provides another interesting illustration of the sealing of the Spirit. For certain types of loads, when a truck is fully loaded and ready for its run, a plastic seal is put around the lock on the door. Breaking this seal before the truck reaches its destination will mean the loss of one's job. This is similar to the sealing of the Spirit. The seal of the Spirit cannot be broken before the Christian reaches his heavenly destination. It is our guarantee of reaching the destination God intends for us.

THINKING BACK

All these ministries of the Holy Spirit to us are simultaneous at the moment of salvation. While the conviction process may be long and drawn-out previous to salvation, we are not saved without it. It is still present at the moment of salvation, convincing us to repent, to turn from our previous attitudes about Christ, and to accept Him as our personal savior. Regeneration, indwelling, baptism, and sealing all occur the moment we say "yes" to the invitation of Christ.

SPEED BUMP!

Slow down to be sure you've gotten the main points of this section.

1. What is conviction?
Conviction is the ministry of the Holy Spirit in which He causes us to recognize our sin and prompts us to turn from it.

2. What is regeneration?
Regeneration is the ministry of the Holy Spirit in which He causes us to be born again spiritually, resulting in eternal life.

3. What is indwelling?
Indwelling is the ministry of the Holy Spirit coming to live in the body of each Christian.

4. What is baptism?

Baptism of the Holy Spirit is the ministry of the Spirit incorporating the Christian into the body of Christ.

5. What is sealing?

Sealing of the Holy Spirit is the ministry of the Spirit marking us as God's own possession and guaranteeing our salvation.

FOR FURTHER STUDY

Scripture Passages

- Psalm 32:3-5
- John 3:3-7
- John 14:16-17
- John 16:8-11
- Romans 6:1-10
- 1 Corinthians 1:13

- 1 Corinthians 6:19
- 2 Corinthians 1:22
- 2 Corinthians 5:17
- Ephesians 4:30
- Titus 3:5

FAQ #13

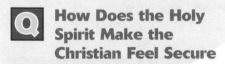

Q **How Does the Holy Spirit Make the Christian Feel Secure**

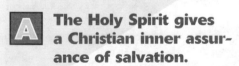

A **The Holy Spirit gives a Christian inner assurance of salvation.**

Central Passage: Romans 8:16, The Spirit Himself bears witness with our spirit that we are children of God.

"A humble, ignorant man or woman depending on the mind of God has an explanation for things that the rational man without the Spirit of God never has."

Oswald Chambers (1874-1917)

There are few things more plaguing than wanting to be a Christian and not being sure you are one. I have already told you of when I became a Christian and all the questions I had at first. As a result of this rather shaky start, for a number of years I was a little weak on assurance of salvation. This was particularly acute whenever I had to fly. It was white-knuckle time from takeoff to landing. Turbulence had a dramatic effect on me. The slightest bump caused my heart to race, my breath to become short. On the outside, I looked calm and unflappable. On the inside, I was shouting, "Oh, God, if you get me off this plane, I'll never get on a plane again as long as I live." But then, the plane would land, everything I had felt and said seemed pretty silly, and eventually I'd get on a plane again, to a repeat performance.

Uncertainty about your salvation can be agonizing.

The Holy Spirit definitely had an uphill battle with me. But, true to His word, He won. He assured me that I was a Christian. First, I read 2 Corinthians 5:17, "If anyone is in Christ, he is a new creation; old things have passed away; behold, all things have become new." I had noticed a number of my more flagrant sins had, without conscious effort on my part, disappeared. I thought that was significant. Then, when I read the Corinthians passage, something deep down inside me shouted, "That's why. I've become a new creation. Old things have passed away, and all things have become new." I'm not sure I had an accurate understanding of the passage, but I began to gain assurance anyway.

Then, I put several passages together that convinced me even more:

Why Do I Need to Know This?

1. To have a biblical view of the ministry of the Holy Spirit.
2. To benefit from His ministry to me and not miss out on anything due to my ignorance.
3. To be able correctly to represent the ministry of the Holy Spirit to others.

1. "There is forgiveness with You" (Psalm 130:4). This gave me hope. It meant forgiveness could be obtained from God.

2. "The one who comes to Me I will by no means cast out" (John 6:37). I had come to Him; there was no doubt about that. I had repented of my sin and asked Jesus to forgive my sin, to come into my life and make me the kind of person He wanted me to be and give me eternal life so I could live with Him in heaven. Since I had come to Him, and He had promised He would not cast me out, clearly I had Jesus.

3. "He who has the Son has life" (1 John 5:12). Because I had the Son, I had eternal life.

The Holy Spirit used these passages to convince me that I was, indeed, a Christian. I finally gained assurance of my salvation through the ministry of the Holy Spirit.

Giving us assurance of our salvation is one of the ministries the Holy Spirit has to us. In Romans 8:15-17, we read, "For you did not receive the spirit of bondage again to fear [when you became Christians], but you received the Spirit of adoption by whom we cry out 'Abba, Father.' The Spirit Himself bears witness with our spirit that we are children of God, and if children, then heirs—heirs of God and joint heirs with Christ, if indeed we suffer with Him, that we may also be glorified together." We gain an inner assurance that we are children of God, and that inner assurance comes from the Holy Spirit. Beyond that, I don't know that we can say how He does it, or if He does it in the same way with each person. In my case, He gave me a clearer understanding of some Scripture passages, which led me to assurance.

A new creation does things differently.

FAQ #14

 How Does the Holy Spirit Teach the Christian?

 The Holy Spirit divinely enables a Christian to understand Scripture in a way that he could not before becoming a Christian.

Central Passage: 1 Corinthians 2:13, These things we also speak, not in words which man's wisdom teaches but which the Holy Spirit teaches.

I struggled spiritually for many months before I became a Christian. I was frustrated with a lack of purpose and meaning in life, I was under terrible guilt for sins I was committing, and I was terribly fearful of dying, because I figured I would go to hell when I died. In my tormented condition, I picked up an old family Bible and tried to read it, but I couldn't make heads or tails of it. It was like trying to read a book on nonsense. I spoke English and the Bible I was reading was written in English, but I got absolutely nothing out of it.

Then, on September 1, 1966, I became a Christian; and the man who led me to the Lord gave me a paperback New Testament and encouraged me to read the Gospel of John several times. When I

picked up the Bible this time, it came alive with meaning. I couldn't get enough of it. I read it over and over, every spare minute I had. I didn't understand everything I read, but I was ecstatic with what I did under-stand. So I read and read, not worrying about what I didn't under-stand, just trying to increase my knowl-edge of what I did. I'm not suggesting everyone will experience this kind of difference upon conversion. But it is an example of the illumining ministry of the Holy Spirit. What was the difference between the first and second times I tried to read the Bible? The second time I had the Holy Spirit living inside me, teaching me, opening my mind to the truth of Scripture, helping me understand. In 1 Corinthians 2:9-10 we read:

**"Eye has not seen, nor ear heard,
Nor have entered into the heart of man
The things which God has prepared for those who love Him."
But God has revealed them to us through His Spirit.**

There we have it. God reveals things to us through His Spirit that we would not know otherwise. He enables us to understand and apply what He has already revealed in the Scriptures. The pull to sin that is within each of us clouds our minds and our wills so that we misunderstand, misinterpret, and resist the full truth of Scripture. We lack both the ability and the inclination to understand. The Holy Spirit, however, opens our minds and warms our hearts so that we have a growing understanding and a growing inclination to follow Scripture (Ephesians 1:17-18; 3:18-19; 2 Corinthians 3:14-16; 4:6). It may not be as sudden and clear-cut as my experience, but the Holy Spirit will open the mind of the Christian to the truth of Scripture. David prayed again and again, especially in Psalm 119, that the Lord would teach Him. "Deal bountifully with Your servant, that I may live and keep Your word. Open my eyes, that I may see wondrous things from Your law" (vv. 17-18). That is a prayer we all can pray. It is a prayer God delights in answering.

While we want to *do*, God wants us to *be*.

FAQ #15

How Does the Holy Spirit Lead and Guide Us?

The Holy Spirit leads and guides Christians by putting it in our hearts and minds to do His will and by providentially governing our circumstances.

Central Passage: **Philippians 2:12-13, Work out your own salvation with fear and trembling; for it is God who works in you both to will and to do for His good pleasure.**

How to know the will of God can be one of the great challenges of the Christian life, and often one of the great frustrations of the young Christian life. The young Christian, in his zeal, wants God to let him know everything that He should do, and God doesn't do that. God's will in the New Testament is primarily moral. He wants us to "be" the right kind of people. If we are the right kind of people, God will find it easy to lead us to do whatever He wants us to do. Typically, however, we are pre-occupied with what God wants us to *do*, when we should be comfortable just being the kind of person God wants us to *be*, and resting in His sovereignty to determine what we should do.

Nevertheless, the Bible does indicate that God will lead us and guide us, even though we may not feel led or guided. Romans 8:14 says, "For as many as are led by the Spirit of God, these are the sons of God." Galatians 5:16, 18 reads, "Walk in the Spirit, and you shall not fulfill the lust of the flesh. But if you are led by the Spirit, you are not under the law." So we see that we are led by the Spirit, or can be, but how? What does that mean?

Of course, the easiest way to be led is by providentially governed circumstances. If circumstances prohibit you from doing something, you know it is not the will of God. He is not leading you into someplace where He makes it impossible to go.

The next easiest way He leads is through Scripture. The Holy Spirit may make a passage of the Bible known to us, and that may lead us or guide us.

A further way is through the counsel of others. Proverbs teaches that there is safety in the multitude of counselors. It takes a brave or foolish person to go counter to an abundance of solid, wise counsel.

Finally, apparently God plants inclinations, thoughts, or desires in our mind to lead and guide us. This is the most subjective and the most dangerous, because it is often difficult to know whether something in our head is our own personal desire, or perhaps even a deception by the evil one. In such a case, it is helpful simply to retrace the above principles. First, do circumstances tell us anything? If you try to go through a door that has been closed by God, you often end up with a sore head. An apparently closed door is not always an indication of the Lord's will, however. It may be for faith-building, or to make sure the timing is right. Second, does the Scripture tell us anything? Third, is there agreement on an abundance of godly wisdom and counsel?

If you love God, you want to please Him.

Finally, if you have followed these steps and you still don't sense any direct leading or guiding from the Lord, you are free to do as you please. The great reformer Martin Luther said, "Love God and do as you please." Of course, this could easily be misunderstood or abused. But what he meant was, if you love God, you will obey His commandments. The apostle John recorded the words of Jesus: "If you love Me, you will keep My commandments" (John 14:15 NASB). If you disobey His commandments, at least for that moment, you have stopped loving God. If you love God, you will not do anything that you understand to be wrong.

Philip Yancey wrote, in a little booklet entitled *Guidance*:

I have a confession to make. For me, at least, guidance only becomes evident when I look backward, months and years later.

Then the circuitous process falls into place and the hand of God seems clear. But at that moment of decision, I feel mainly confusion and uncertainty. Indeed, almost all the guidance in my life has been subtle and indirect.

This pattern has recurred so often (and clear guidance for the future has occurred so seldom) that I am about to conclude that we have a basic direction wrong. I had always thought of guidance as forward-looking. We keep praying, hoping, counting on God to reveal what we should do next. In my own experience, at least, I have found the direction to be reversed. The focus must be on the moment before me, the present. How is my relationship to God? As circumstances change, for better or worse, will I respond with obedience and trust?

God does guide—sometimes through an inner conviction, sometimes through circumstances, sometimes through Scripture or godly counsel. But sometimes we don't have any sense of being led or guided. That does not mean we aren't. It means we are free to love God and do as we please, and wait to see, in retrospect, what the will of God was.

FAQ #16

 How Does the Holy Spirit Help Us Pray?

 The Holy Spirit encourages and enables us to pray, and even prays to God the Father for us when we don't know what to pray.

Central Passage: Romans 8:26-27, The Spirit also helps in our weaknesses. For we do not know what we should pray for as we ought, but the Spirit Himself makes intercession for us with groanings which cannot be uttered. Now [God the Father] who searches the hearts knows what the mind of the Spirit is, because [the Spirit] makes intercession for the saints according to the will of God.

In a Peanuts cartoon many years ago, Linus told Lucy, "I've made an important theological discovery. If you hold your hands upside down when you pray, you get the opposite of what you prayed for."

Many of us read that and think, "So that's what's the matter with my prayers. I've been holding my hands upside down!" Certainly there are times when we get the opposite of what we prayed for. Prayer is one of the most difficult problems in the Christian life.

The Bible suggests that the Holy Spirit encourages us and guides us in our prayer (Ephesians 6:18; Jude 20). Yet there are times, the Bible says, when we do not know how to pray as we should (Romans 8:26, NASB), but we already knew that from experience. First, the Bible says whatever we ask in Jesus' name, it will be given to us (John 14:13). But then, it says we must ask in faith without doubting (James 1:6), without unconfessed sin (John 9:31), and in God's will (1 John 5:14). Well, what if we don't know what God's will is? What do we do then?

> **We can pray freely, knowing the Holy Spirit is praying for us.**

Our purpose in this chapter is not to answer all the questions we might have about prayer. Rather, our purpose is to make this point: The Holy Spirit wants us to pray, encourages us to pray, guides us in prayer, and when we do not know what to pray for, the Holy Spirit takes up our cause and prays to the Father for us. Therefore, we should never fear praying to God or be discouraged about our prayer. Rather, we can go to God and admit that we don't know how to pray for something as we ought, and rest in the confidence that the Holy Spirit will make the proper prayer on our behalf. What freedom that gives us! We can just pray, with a free heart, knowing that the Holy Spirit is praying for us at the same time, translating our mixed-up thoughts, our uncertainty and ignorance, into valid, meaningful prayers.

The Scripture makes it clear that we are not to pray with selfish motives (James 4:3), or with sin in our heart (Psalm 66:18), or without faith (James 1:6). At the same time, God readily hears the prayer, "Lord, I have sinned. Forgive my sin, and restore me to fellowship with you." If we have taken care of those matters, we can pray. So pray. Risk praying poorly. Pray the best you know how. The Holy Spirit is there, translating, interpreting, praying to the Father for you.

SPEED BUMP!

Slow down to be sure you've gotten the main points of this section.

1. **How does the Holy Spirit make the Christian feel secure?**
The Holy Spirit gives a Christian inner assurance of salvation.

2. **How does the Holy Spirit teach the Christian?**
The Holy Spirit divinely enables a Christian to understand Scripture in a way that he could not before becoming a Christian.

3. **How does the Holy Spirit lead and guide us?**
The Holy Spirit leads and guides Christians by putting it in our hearts and minds to do His will and by providentially governing our circumstances.

4. **How does the Holy Spirit help us pray?**
The Holy Spirit encourages and enables us to pray, and even prays to God the Father for us when we don't know what to pray.

FOR FURTHER STUDY

Scripture Passages

- Psalm 119:17-18
- Romans 8:14-16
- Romans 8:26-27
- 1 Corinthians 2:6-10
- 2 Corinthians 3:14-16
- 2 Corinthians 4:6
- Galatians 5:16-18
- Ephesians 1:17-18
- Ephesians 3:18-19
- Philippians 2:12-13
- 1 John 2:27

FAQ #17

 What Is the Goal of Spiritual Change?

 The goal of spiritual change is transformation into the spiritual likeness of Jesus.

Central Passage: 2 Corinthians 3:18, But we all, with unveiled face, beholding as in a mirror the glory of the Lord, are being transformed into the same image from glory to glory, just as by the Spirit of the Lord.

An old proverb says, "The apple never falls far from the tree." It means that children are often like their parents, both physically and in some nonphysical characteristics. God also wants us to not fall far from His tree. His goal for us as Christians is that we be changed from our pre-Christian nature into the likeness of Jesus. In our central passage, we see that we are being transformed by the Spirit of the Lord into the image of Jesus. Romans 12:1-2 says essentially the same thing: "I beseech you therefore, brethren, by the mercies of God, that you present your bodies a living sacrifice, holy, acceptable to God, which is your reasonable service. And do not be conformed to this world, but be transformed by the renewing of your mind,

"Without the present illumination of the Holy Spirit, the Word of God must remain a dead letter to every man, no matter how intelligent or well-educated he may be. It is just as essential for the Holy Spirit to reveal the truth of Scripture to the reader today as it was necessary for him to inspire the writers in their day."

William Law (1686-1761)

that you may prove what is that good and acceptable and perfect will of God."

To understand this passage better, try working it backwards. If we
want to be a living demonstration (proof) of the fact that God's will is
good and acceptable and perfect, we must be transformed. To be transformed, we must have our mind renewed. To have our mind
renewed, we must present ourselves to God as a living sacrifice.
This, then, is our goal—the spiritual likeness of
Jesus. What is the spiritual likeness of Jesus? You
are to love God with "all your heart, with all
your soul, and with all your mind. This is
the first and great commandment. And
the second is like it: You shall love your neighbor as yourself." That is the opening picture of
what it means to be like Jesus. It means you love God
and your fellow-man.

God wants us to be more like Jesus.

You might ask, however, how you love God. The Gospel of
John answers that clearly: "If you love me, keep My commandments"
(John 14:15). The essence of loving God is not sweeping emotions or
lofty intentions; it is obedience. Regardless of our emotions or our good
intentions, if we do not keep God's commandments, we cannot say we
love Him. By this I do not mean a casual type of obedience, but obedience from the heart because we believe God always has our best in mind.

Two other passages help give us a picture of the image of Jesus and a
glimpse of what it means to love our neighbor. One is 1 Corinthians
13:4-7: "Love suffers long and is kind; love does not envy; love does not
parade itself, is not puffed up; does not behave rudely, does not seek its
own, is not provoked, thinks no evil; does not rejoice in iniquity, but
rejoices in the truth." That is what it means to love others.

To let this passage have its full impact, put your own name in
the blank, in place of the word "love." (Your name) suffers long

and is kind; _____ does not envy; _____ does not
parade [himself], is not puffed up; _____ does not behave
rudely, does not seek his own, is not provoked, thinks no evil;
_____ does not rejoice in iniquity, but rejoices in the truth.
How did you do? How close are you to the image of Christ
using this passage as a yardstick?

All these passages together do not give us the total picture, but
they put us well on our way to understanding what it means to be
like Jesus. We love God and we love others. It's a big task.

FAQ #18

 What Is at the Heart of Spiritual Change?

 **At the heart of spiritual change is an interac-
tion in which the Holy Spirit prompts and the
individual responds.**

Central Passage: **Philippians 2:12-13, Work out your own salvation with fear and trembling; for it is God who works in you
both to will and to do for His good pleasure.**

Like many things in the Bible, spiritual growth can seem fairly
simple on the surface, but when you plumb the depths, it becomes
extremely complex. While we may never understand everything about
spiritual change in the Christian, our central passage in Philippians
suggests that God places a thought or desire in our mind—it may be
a conviction that something we have done is wrong, or that we ought
to do something positive—and we either respond or reject that
thought or desire. If we nourish His divine "seed," that encourages
more, and if we extinguish it, that encourages less.

The Holy Spirit may put into our mind a command from
Scripture as we are tempted to sin. He may give us an impulse to
do something kind for someone in need. It might be a feeling of

remorse over something we said, and a conviction that we ought to ask for forgiveness. If we respond positively to that inner prompting, we are strengthened by the Spirit for the next test. If we respond negatively, we are weakened by our flesh (Romans 7:18-25) for the next test. If we develop a habit of responding positively, we develop a strong Christian charac-ter. Negative responses lead to a weak Christian character. On the surface, it seems as simple as that.

God initiates a positive impulse, and we respond.

Below the surface, it is much more complicated, however, because our ability to understand Scripture is a result of the work of the Holy Spirit in our lives (1 Corinthians 2:9-15). Furthermore, our ability to bear any fruit in the Christian life is dependent on Jesus ("for without Me you can do nothing," John 15:5).

Ephesians 2:8-9 says, "For by grace you have been saved through faith, and that not of yourselves; it is the gift of God, not of works, lest anyone should boast." The question we must ask about this pas-sage is, "To what does the 'that' refer?" Does it mean the grace to be saved is not of ourselves? Or does it mean the faith to be saved is not of ourselves? The word nearest to "that" is "faith." Normally, the word "that" refers to the thing closest to it. So, if the passage teaches that even the faith to be saved is not of ourselves, but is a gift of God, it only adds to the mystery of spiritual growth. If that which we need to be saved and grow spiritually is given us by God, how, then, can be we held accountable to be more than we are, spiritually? And yet, the Bible holds us accountable for our spiritual growth (Romans 6:1-14).

We cannot solve the mystery. All we can do is live in the light of what we understand. We understand this much: God somehow puts thoughts, desires, Scriptures, convictions, or impulses into our minds ("it is God who works in you both to will and to do for His good pleas-ure"). We are responsible to act properly on them ("work out your own salvation with fear and trembling"). When we do, God increases our capacity to respond positively the next time. When we don't, our capaci-ty to respond positively the next time is diminished. As we say "yes" to God, He makes us stronger spiritually. As we say "no" to Him, we make ourselves weaker.

The principle of Matthew 25:15-29 makes it clear that light received brings more light, and light rejected brings greater darkness; obedience now makes greater obedience possible in the future.

How do we grow, spiritually? The grace of God is the basis of all spiritual growth. But, because we do not have the luxury of being totally passive in this process, it is helpful to observe how God sometimes works in our lives. The Holy Spirit puts something in our mind. We respond positively, as best we know how, as fully as we are able. The Lord accepts our positive heart response as a proper act of faith and enables us to respond on a level that He determines. This strengthens us for greater response next time. His grace makes possible our obedience and our growth.

The fruit of the Spirit, we learn in Galatians 5:22-23, is love, joy, peace, longsuffering, kindness, goodness, faithfulness, gentleness, and self-control. If these are the fruits of the Spirit, they are not the fruit of self-effort. That means that we cannot create them in our own lives. The Holy Spirit must create them. Yet, the Holy Spirit will not

Why Do I Need to Know This?

1. If I don't know that transformation into the spiritual image of Jesus is God's primary goal for me, I may misunderstand His work in my life, especially wondering why He does not make life easier for His follower.

2. If I don't understand that spiritual growth is an interaction between me and the Holy Spirit, I may fall into one of two errors. I may put too much emphasis on my own responsibility, or, I may put too much emphasis on God's sovereignty.

3. If I don't understand all the elements of God's spiritual transformation process, I may leave out one or more in my mind, and either stunt my spiritual growth or get frustrated because I don't understand why my growth isn't progressing more quickly.

create this fruit in our lives unless we are pursuing the things that encourage this fruit.

We should be aware of the danger inherent in following inner impulses, namely that you might get an inner impulse that is not from God. Where would the impulse come from? Two sources are possible: the human mind or demonic forces. The human mind, unaided by the Holy Spirit, can create inner impulses. Non-Christians have "hunches" all the time. Also, it is clear that the devil is capable of moving us to do things (1 Chronicles 21:1). So we must not blindly follow our inner impulses.

Early in my ministry I knew of a lady with a painful and chronic condition who became a Christian. She prayed to God continuously to take the pain away. One day, it came into her mind that she should go to a certain drugstore in the city that was unknown to her. She was to ask the druggist for a certain kind of medication that, again, was unknown to her. She did these things. But the druggist told her that medicine was not even manufactured anymore. The woman was crushed. She felt God had lied to her. She turned from God, and though this was many years ago, the last I knew, she was still rejecting the Lord.

What went wrong with that experience? How is someone to know if an inner impulse is from God or not? Well, frankly, it is like much of life. The will of God becomes clear after the fact, not before. There are many times when we do not know what the will of God is. We make the best decision we know how at the time, and later we gain perspective. Someone once observed, "Life is lived forward, but understood backward."

Several principles can help us evaluate our inner impulses.

1. One of my pastors early in my Christian experience often said, "Follow your good impulses. It is probably the Holy Spirit." If the impulse is to do something good, there is little danger in doing it. In fact, it really doesn't matter if the impulse is directly from the Holy Spirit or indirectly from God through your spiritually influenced mind, if good is the result. We are to do good to others anyway (Galatians 6:10).

2. Sometimes the impulse is to do something that seems neither good nor bad. If it is a small thing, it is not necessary to agonize over it. Do it if you want to. In 1 Corinthians 10:27, Paul wrote, "If any of those who do not believe invites you to dinner, and you desire to go, eat whatever is set before you, asking no question for conscience' sake." It does not say "Pray about it, get counsel from ten people, and then wait twenty-four hours before making your final decision." It simply says, "If you want to go, go."

If it is a big thing, then you will want to pray about it, seek counsel, search the Scriptures, and make a pro and con list. Don't do any big thing hastily.

3. Trust in the character of God. The woman who turned her back on God over the drugstore incident revealed a deep flaw in her understanding of God. If you believe that God is all-good, all-powerful, and all-knowing, then you can trust Him. The proper response to that lady's inner impulse might have been to go to the drugstore and ask for the medicine, but when she learned that the medicine was no longer manufactured, to cast herself on God's character and admit that the process of inner impulses is an imperfect one, or to admit that the inner impulse might have just come from her subconscious mind. The impulse might also have come as a test from Satan, in which case prayer to the Lord for protection from his deception would be in order.

I think that the more spiritually mature a person is, the more he can trust such impulses. The less mature he is, the more caution should be exercised. In all cases, caution is the watchword.

FAQ #19

What Process Must We Go Through to Become Like Christ?

To become like Christ requires the combination of the work of God, the word of God, personal commitment, other believers, and time and trials.

Central Passage: Romans 12:1-2. I beseech you therefore, brethren, by the mercies of God, that you present your bodies a living sacrifice, holy, acceptable to God, which is your reasonable service. And do not be conformed to this world, but be transformed by the renewing of your mind, that you may prove what is that good and acceptable and perfect will of God.

Five key ingredients are required for someone to develop a mature Christian character. They are the work of God, the word of God, personal commitment, other believers, and time and trials.

The Work of God

As we saw earlier, it is God who works in us "both to will and to do for His good pleasure." Someone has said, "God does the work of God, and man does the work of man. Man *cannot* do the work of God, and God *will not* do the work of man." If that is the case, we must be clear about what is the work of God and what is our responsibility. We have a great genius for turning the two around. We prefer to try to do the work of God and neglect the work of man. It doesn't work. We must look to God to initiate the work in our hearts, and we must respond with faithful obedience.

The Word of God

Transformation cannot be complete without the word of God. Without the Bible, we don't know what we should do, and the Holy Spirit does not have His key tool in our lives. The writer of the Book of Hebrews wrote: "[God's word] is full of living power: it is sharper than the sharpest dagger, cutting swift and deep into our innermost thoughts and desires…exposing us for what we really are" (4:12 LB).

The Scripture has inherent power as it is used by the Holy Spirit in our lives. The apostle Paul wrote: "All Scripture is given by inspiration of God, and is profitable for doctrine, for reproof, for correction, for instruction in righteousness, that the man of God may be complete, thoroughly equipped for every good work" (2 Timothy 3:16-17).

David wrote in the Psalms, "How can a young man cleanse his way? By taking heed according to Your word…Your word I have hidden in my heart, that I might not sin against You…Your word is a lamp to my feet and a light to my path" (Psalm 119:9, 11, 105). He also wrote, in Psalm 19, that the word of God was more valuable than gold, sweeter than honey, and by it "Your servant is warned, and in keeping them there is great reward."

Without the Scriptures, no one has a hope of always making wise decisions, of consistently discerning the will of God, of knowing how to sustain relationships, of having a morally tuned conscience, of knowing right from wrong in the small as well as great areas of life, of knowing God well and worshiping Him in spirit and in truth, or of being equipped to live and minister in this world. In addition to the work of God, it takes the word of God to become spiritually mature.

Personal Commitment

Spiritual growth requires personal commitment. As we have already seen, spiritual growth is an interaction between the Christian and the Holy Spirit. The Christian cannot be totally passive in the process. God will not pull a Christian out of bed in the morning, splash cold water in his face, brew him a cup of coffee, and sit him down in front of his Bible. The Christian must do that himself. We must be personally involved in the pursuit of righteousness. Paul wrote in 1 Corinthians 9:24-27, "Do you not know that those who run in a race all run, but one receives the prize?

Run in such a way that you may obtain it. And everyone who competes for the prize is temperate in all things. Now they do it to obtain a perishable crown, but we for an imperishable crown. Therefore I run thus: not with uncertainty. Thus I fight: not as one who beats the air. But I discipline my body and bring it into subjection, lest, when I have preached to others, I myself should become disqualified." Yes, personal commitment is one key to spiritual transformation.

Other Believers

Spiritual transformation does not happen in isolation. We need the ministry of other believers in our lives. The Christian life was never designed to be lived in isolation. The Lone Ranger is not a role model for Christians. The Three Musketeers would be more like it— all for one and one for all. The apostle Paul wrote in Ephesians 4:11-13, 15-16,

And He Himself gave some to be apostles, some prophets, some evangelists, and some pastors and teachers, for the equipping of the saints for the work of ministry, for the edifying of the body of Christ, till we all come to the unity of the faith and of the knowledge of the Son of God, to a perfect man, to the measure of the stature of the fullness of Christ...but, speaking the truth in love, [we] may grow up in all things into Him who is the head—Christ—from whom the whole body, joined and knit together by what every joint supplies, according to the effective working by which every part does its share, causes growth of the body for the edifying of itself in love.

We are gifted and called by God to live a life intertwined with other Christians, so that we can all help one another grow to spiritual maturity. We cannot do it alone. God has seen to that.

Time and Trials

Finally, time and trials are necessary for spiritual transformation. No one was ever holy in a hurry. Paul writes in 1 Timothy that an elder must not be a new convert, lest he become conceited and fall into the snare of the devil (3:6 NASB). Peter calls new Christians "babes" and declares that they must drink milk in order to grow spiritually, to the point at which they can begin to eat solid food (Hebrews 5:12-14). All this implies that, when compared with physical growth, spiritual transformation takes time.

No one was ever holy in a hurry.

It also takes trials. No one ever grew to maturity on a cloud of ease. In fact, the writer of the Book of Hebrews speaks of the need for God's children to be disciplined, just as earthly fathers discipline earthly children, and that if we do not receive discipline from God, it is a sign that we are not His children (Hebrews 12:8). He goes on to say that "no chastening seems to be joyful for the present, but painful; nevertheless afterward it yields the peaceable fruit of righteousness to those who have been trained by it" (12:11).

In a similar line of thought, the apostle James wrote, "My brethren, count it all joy when [not if] you fall into various trials, knowing that the testing of your faith produces patience. But let patience have its perfect work, that you may be perfect and complete, lacking nothing" (1:2-4).

Do you want the peaceable fruit of righteousness? You can have it. Respond properly to the chastening of God in your life. Do you want to be mature, lacking in nothing? You can be. Respond properly to the trials that will come into your life.

The process of growing into Christlikeness requires the work of God, the word of God, personal commitment, other believers, and time and trials.

FAQ #20

Q **Why Don't We Change More Quickly and More Completely?**

A **We don't change more quickly and more completely because God has decreed that we be transformed over time and because of the complications of sin.**

Central Passage: 1 Peter 2:2, As newborn babes, desire the pure milk of the word, that you may grow thereby.

We have made several allusions to this question, but it will be helpful to stop and talk about it. We all wish we were farther down the road spiritually than we are. Why don't we change more quickly, and why isn't our change more all-encompassing? Why do I change in one area and not another? The bottom line is, "I don't know." But let's speculate together for a moment. There are three things to consider.

God Is a Picturing God

All spiritual truth is pictured by something physical. Death and resurrection, for example, are pictured by the seasons. In fall, the earth begins to die until, by winter, it is dead. In spring, new life begins to stir, and in summer the resurrection of the globe is complete. In another example, the Old Testament sacrificial system is a picture of the spiritual atonement that Jesus accomplished for us. Again, marriage is a picture of the relationship that Christians will have with Jesus in heaven. God is a picturing God.

God has given us a picture in the process of human physical life. A person is born a helpless infant, totally dependent on others for his needs. Through proper care and nourishment, he begins to grow physically and mentally. The person progresses from infancy to childhood to youth to adulthood. The same thing happens spiritually. When someone becomes a Christian, the Bible says he is "born again" (John 3:7). As a new child, he must drink spiritual milk, continue to grow, and progress to the point at which he can eat spiritual solid food (Hebrews 5:12-14).

A physical child can see adults and want to be like them. So can a spiritual child. A physical child stretches, fails, tries again, fails, and tries again. So does a spiritual child. When I was a child, basketball was my passion. My older brother was a good player, and I was consumed by a desire to be like him. I used to jump and jump around the house. When I was ten or twelve, I would try to jump and touch the kitchen ceiling. When I could touch it, I then wanted to be able to hit it with the palm of my hand. Then, my goal was to get my elbow that high, and, finally, my head. I was a compulsive jumper, never satisfied with how high I could jump or how tall I was. My mother is a saint for having put up with me (though she once made me wash the dirty finger streaks off the kitchen ceiling).

> **O**ur physical growth "pictures" our spiritual growth.

God intended us to "grow," not "poof" into maturity. The fact that we grow slowly physically and want to be more than we are and do more than we can physically is merely a picture of the same spiritual truth.

Limitations

When I was growing up, I had injuries, illness, and other inherent limitations. I had ankle and knee injuries that limited my potential. I never got as tall as I wanted to be and never jumped as high as I wanted to jump. Why? Because I was limited by the genes I inherited, and because the Fall of humanity resulted in things like disease and accidents. Some of my accidents have left permanent limitations. The same is true spiritually. The Fall results in our being susceptible to spiritual disease and accidents, and we have inherent limitations. I cannot be the second Billy Graham. I am not gifted or called to be. I have permanent spiritual scars from things in my past. I have permanent spiritual weaknesses. I may be strong where you are weak. I may be weak where you are strong. That is simply the way it is. Because of God's plan to have us "grow" rather than "poof" into maturity, and because of the effects of the Fall and sin in our lives, we will never be all that we want to be on this side of heaven

The Grace of God

Despite our limitations, God's grace covers all our sins. God's love overcomes all our shortcomings. God "knows our frame; He is mindful that we are but dust" (Psalm 103:14 NASB). Plus, we are not yet what we are going to be. God is not finished with us yet. He will ultimately perfect us in every regard when we join Him in heaven. Until then, we must be satisfied with the fact that, in the eyes of God, because of Jesus, we are perfect.

SPEED BUMP!

Slow down to be sure you've gotten the main points of this section.

1. What is the goal of spiritual change?
The goal of spiritual change is transformation into the spiritual likeness of Jesus.

2. What is at the heart of spiritual change?
At the heart of spiritual change is an interaction in which the Holy Spirit prompts and the individual responds.

3. What process must we go through to become like Christ?
To become like Christ requires the combination of the work of God, the word of God, personal commitment, other believers, and time and trials.

4. Why don't we change more quickly and more completely?
We don't change more quickly and more completely because God has decreed that we be transformed over time and because of the complications of sin.

FOR FURTHER STUDY

Scripture Passages

- John 15:5
- Romans 6:1-14
- Romans 7:18-25
- Romans 12:1-2

- Galatians 5:22-23
- Ephesians 2:8-9
- Philippians 2:12-13
- Hebrews 5:12-14

FAQ #21

 What Is a Spiritual Gift?

 A spiritual gift is a God-given ability for ministry to others.

Central Passage: 1 Peter 4:10, As each one has received a gift, minister it to one another, as good stewards of the manifold grace of God.

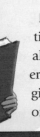

Not only do we differ in natural gifts and abilities, but the Bible teaches us that each Christian also has been given a spiritual gift, or possibly several spiritual gifts. Only Christians have spiritual gifts, because the Holy Spirit gives these gifts and only does so after He comes to dwell within the believer (1 Corinthians 12:11). These are not just finely honed natural abilities; they are special God-given abilities to minister to others. Sometimes they correspond closely with our natural talents, but they are more than just talents.

> "If we prune back that part of our activity which is not really fruitful in the Holy Spirit, we find that we do less, but accomplish more."
>
> *John Michael Talbot*

The Bible has much to say about spiritual gifts, but there are many different interpretations of the information. In researching for this chapter, I have read several books, consulted a number of others, and received a summary of research from a rather large selection of books on the Holy Spirit. It is safe to say that no two of the books agree on all things. The best we can say is that people tend to fall into one of several "camps." One camp generally believes that "miraculous" spiritual gifts still exist as they did in the Bible, and the other camp generally doesn't.

I cannot offer a definitive treatment of spiritual gifts that will answer all the questions. There are some clear areas of agreement, however, and we should look at those before we look at the areas where perspectives differ.

First, each Christian has a spiritual gift. First Peter 4:10 says, "each one." Paul writes in 1 Corinthians 12:7, "each one." Romans 12:3 says "each one." Each one of us has a spiritual gift.

Second, the gifts are to be used in love. First Peter 4:8 says we are to "have fervent love for one another," as we minister our gift to others (4:10). Romans 12:10 says that we must be "kindly affectionate to one another with brotherly love, in honor giving preference for one another," as we use our spiritual gifts (Romans 12:4-6). First Corinthians 12:7 teaches that the use of our spiritual gifts must be "for the profit of all."

Third, the gifts are for the benefit of one another, as has already been stated or implied. First Peter 4:10 says, "Minister...to *one another*." Romans 12:5 says, "We, being many, are one body in Christ, and individually members of *one another*," and therefore, minister to one another. Ephesians 4:12 says that our gifts are "for the equipping of the saints for the work of ministry, for the edifying of *the body of Christ*." (Italics added.)

We see, then, that the spiritual gifts that we all have are not for the purpose of building up or advancing ourselves, but for serving

I need to know that I have a spiritual gift, or I may fail not only to serve the Lord as effectively as I might but also to enjoy my service to Him as fully as He wants me to. There are some gifts I will never have, but all Christians need each other as we live in a context of mutual ministry.

one another in love. We are to use our spiritual gift; it is an obligation.

In talking about spiritual gifts, I have chosen three terms that are not in the Bible, but which I have found helpful in understanding spiritual gifts. Those terms are "office gifts," "service gifts," and "special gifts." A person, for example, with the office gift of pastor-teacher might have the service gift of teaching.

FAQ #22

 What Are the Office Gifts?

 Office gifts are given to those who serve the church at large in a specific capacity: apostle, prophet, evangelist, and pastor-teacher.

Central Passage: Ephesians 4:11-12, And He Himself gave some to be apostles, some prophets, some evangelists, and some pastors and teachers, for the equipping of the saints for the work of ministry, for the edifying of the body of Christ.

There are three primary categories of spiritual gifts in the New Testament, each one called by a different name. The office gifts are introduced by the Greek word *domata*. It refers to individuals who are gifted and called by God to play the determinative role in establishing, increasing, and overseeing the church. The first two offices, apostles and prophets, seem to have been foundational gifts of the early church that, many believe, disappeared after the church was established. Ephesians 2:20 says that the household of God, the church, was "built on the foundation of the apostles and prophets, Jesus Christ Himself being the chief cornerstone."

Ephesians 2:21-22 goes on to say, "in whom [Jesus] the whole building [the church], being fitted together, grows into a holy temple in the Lord, in whom you also are being built together for a dwelling place of God in the Spirit." This means that after the cornerstone was laid (Jesus' teachings, life, death, resurrection, and ascension), then the rest of the foundation was laid by the apostles and prophets.

Then, the rest of history, from then until the present day, sees a great superstructure being added, and that superstructure is the totality of all Christians from the time of Christ's first coming until He comes again.

The gifted individuals who are called by God to oversee the building of that superstructure are evangelists and pastor-teachers. These, then, are the office gifts. The first two seem to have been temporary, and the last two seem to be permanent.

Each Christian has a gift from the Holy Spirit.

An alternative view sees Jesus to be the keystone, as the critical last stone that holds the stones of an arch in place, or the "head of the corner" (Psalm 118:22), the stone placed at the top of the structure to tie two walls together at the corner. Between the foundation of the apostles and prophets of the earliest church and the exalted Lord as the keystone, the church grows up unto Christ. The image brings together a literal temple building with that of a living being that continues to grow, with Christ as the exalted Head.

Among those who hold this view are many Pentecostal, charismatic, and "third wave" Christians, whose views are explained more fully in the next chapter. These believe that all New Testament gifts continue to operate in the church until Christ's return, including the ministries, or the offices, of apostle and prophet. They agree, however, that first-generation apostles were unique in their direct commissioning from the risen Lord and in their authority to define and establish the gospel and doctrine for the church for all time. Their unique authority had two important results: (1) making clear that the gospel was not just for Jews, but for all who believed in Christ; and (2) the writing of New Testament Scripture. Apart from this important uniqueness, those who believe that all gifts remain in effect until Christ's return believe that modern-day apostles are those God uses to extend the work of the church remarkably, opening fields to the gospel and overseeing larger sections of the body of Christ.

FAQ #23

What Are the Service Gifts?

Service gifts are nonmiraculous gifts that correspond to ministries that all of us should do, but some individuals are gifted for greater impact in those ministries.

Central Passage: **Romans 12:6-8, Having then gifts differing according to the grace that is given to us, let us use them: if prophecy, let us prophesy in proportion to our faith; or ministry, let us use it in our ministering; he who teaches, in teaching; he who exhorts, in exhortation; he who gives, with liberality; he who leads, with diligence; he who shows mercy, with cheerfulness.**

A second kind of spiritual gift is introduced in the New Testament by the Greek word *charismaton.* While there are non-miraculous gifts mentioned in 1 Corinthians 12, the third major passage discussing spiritual gifts, the Romans 12 passage remains the central passage for nonmiraculous gifts. "Prophecy" in Romans 12, for reasons that I will go into later, probably does not mean the ability to predict the future, but rather the powerful proclamation of the word of God. In addition to prophecy, we see the service gifts of ministering (serving or helping), teaching, exhorting, giving, leading, and mercy. There is no biblical definition of these gifts, but general definitions of the gifts seem rather self-evident:

1. Prophecy: the supernatural ability to proclaim the word of God to others.

2. Helping: the supernatural ability to serve, support, and sustain others in need.

3. **Teaching:** the supernatural ability to help others understand the truths of the word of God.

4. **Exhorting:** the supernatural ability to encourage and challenge others.

5. **Giving:** the supernatural ability to meet the physical (mainly financial) needs of others.

6. **Leading:** the supernatural ability to motivate others to pursue a worthy goal.

7. **Mercy:** the supernatural ability to show love and compassion to others.

Few question that these gifts are in force today. A few debate it, but only a few. Most agree that these service gifts are alive and well in the church. While only certain people are gifted by God in these areas (one person might have the gifts of mercy and giving, another person might have the gift of teaching, etc.), all of us are responsible to function in these areas.

Spiritual gift: Prophecy
Command to all: "Go into all the world and preach [proclaim] the gospel to all creation." Mark 16:15 (NASB)

Spiritual gift: Helping
Command to all: "In everything I showed you that by working hard in this manner you must help the weak." Acts 20:35 (NASB)

Spiritual gift: Teaching
Command to all: "Go therefore...teaching them to observe all things that I have commanded you." Matthew 28:19-20

Spiritual gift: Exhortation
Command to all: "Not forsaking our own assembling together...but encouraging one another." Hebrews 10:25 (NASB)

Spiritual gift: Giving
Command to all: "Let each one give as he purposes in his heart, not grudgingly or of necessity; for God loves a cheerful giver." 2 Corinthians 9:7

Spiritual gift: Leading

Command to all: "You also became imitators of us and of the Lord, having received the word in much tribulation with the joy of the Holy Spirit, so that you became an example to all the believers in Macedonia and in Achaia." 1 Thessalonians 1:6-7 (NASB)

Spiritual gift: Mercy

Command to all: "Blessed are the merciful, for they shall obtain mercy." Matthew 5:7

FAQ #24

 What Are Special Gifts?

 Special gifts are miraculous or supernormal gifts that appear to be given for the purpose not only of meeting a need of the moment but also for validating the message of Christianity to those who have not heard or believed.

Central Passage: 1 Corinthians 12:7-11, But the manifestation of the Spirit is given to each one for the profit of all: for to one is given the word of wisdom through the Spirit, to another the word of knowledge through the same Spirit, to another faith by the same Spirit, to another gifts of healings by the same Spirit, to another the working of miracles, to another prophecy, to another discerning of spirits, to another different kinds of tongues, to another the interpretation of tongues. But one and the same Spirit works all these things, distributing to each one individually as He wills.

The third category of gifts is introduced by the Greek word *phanerosis*, which means a "manifestation" (1 Corinthians 12:7). These gifts are supernatural, above and beyond any normal ability. Healing people, speaking in unknown tongues, interpreting what was said in the unknown tongue, performing miracles—all would have to be considered beyond the normal daily routine for most people. Again, no biblical definitions exist, but we can take an educated guess at what they mean:

1. **Word of wisdom: the supernatural ability to discern the wisdom of God for a given situation.**
2. **Word of knowledge: the supernatural ability to know something that is true, such as something that may happen in the future.**
3. **Faith: the supernatural ability to exercise great faith in a situation.**
4. **Healing: the supernatural ability to heal people of physical maladies.**
5. **Miracles: the supernatural ability to perform various miracles.**
6. **Prophecy: the supernatural ability to proclaim the word of God with power and to predict the future.**
7. **Discerning of spirits: the supernatural ability to determine the presence or influence of evil spirits.**
8. **Tongues: the supernatural ability to speak in unknown languages.**
9. **Interpretation: the supernatural ability to give the meaning of an utterance of an unknown tongue.**

The exercise of these gifts often met the immediate needs of those with physical maladies or other pressing needs. In other cases, the exercise of these gifts is said to build up Christians (1 Corinthians 14:4-5, 22); yet in Hebrews 2:4, they are said to have been for the purpose of validating the new message of salvation by grace through faith in Jesus.

As we will see later, Christians differ as to whether or not God intends these special gifts to operate today. Pentecostal, charismatic, and "third wave" Christians believe that these gifts were given to the church until Christ returns. They would also emphasize that these gifts are themselves dimensions of the gospel of Christ expressed in deeds and not just signs that point to a gospel that is separate from the deeds themselves. For example, God's gift of healing a sick person (whether by the earthly Jesus or by the ascended Jesus who heals now through His church) comes not merely to validate or prove the truth that believers are saved by God's grace through faith in Jesus. Instead, such a gift actually demonstrates God's saving grace (the healing is a grace-gift) and is itself one dimension of the salvation set in process by Jesus in His earthly ministry. This process continues through His church until His return, when the many dimensions of salvation are complete and all pain, sorrow, crying, and death pass away (Revelation 21:3-5). This view is discussed more fully in the next section.

O**ur gifts become apparent as we use them.**

THINKING BACK

This is probably the place to note that no list of spiritual gifts in the Bible is the same. Rather than a fixed, exclusive list of gifts with technical definitions, it seems we have been given a representative list of gifts. Common sense will indicate how the gifts are to function. If our list is representative, then it is possible that other gifts exist. For example, some people have a remarkable gift for hospitality; their homes are always open to people for ministry of one kind or another. And, in the New Testament, we are encouraged to be hospitable. If someone said he thought he had the gift of hospitality, I would not quarrel with that possibility from what I understand of Scripture.

In addition, we are never *commanded* to know our gift. Concerning the office gifts, the gift of an evangelist or pastor-teacher will eventually become apparent. Those who evangelize or shepherd and teach with an inner compulsion (in the right sense of the word) will see results that are not experienced by those who do not have such a gift.

We are all instructed to do all the things in the list of service gifts. As we do all those things, experience will reveal what our gift is. Our gift is usually the thing that we see the most clearly, have the greatest burden for, enjoy doing most, and in which we see the most results.

Concerning the special gifts, 1 Corinthians 12:11 says that the Spirit distributes these individually as He wills, and they are so out of the ordinary that if someone had a special gift, it would be clear to all.

The Bible talks much more about our responsibility to live in love and compassion toward others than about focusing on our gifts. As we try to manifest the character of Christ and proclaim His name to others, our gift usually will become apparent. Even if it doesn't, that is no major problem. However, it can be helpful to study the spiritual gifts and get guidance if it is available, to help assess what our gift might be. That way, we might be spared the trauma of trying to function in an area in which we are not gifted or may even be weak.

SPEED BUMP!

Slow down to be sure you've gotten the main points of this section.

1. What is a spiritual gift?
A spiritual gift is a God-given ability for ministry to others.

2. What are the office gifts?
Office gifts are given to those who serve the church at large in a specific capacity: apostle, prophet, evangelist, and pastor-teacher.

3. What are the service gifts?
Service gifts are nonmiraculous gifts that correspond to ministries that all of us should do, but some individuals are gifted for greater impact in those ministries.

4. What are special gifts?
Special gifts are miraculous or supernormal gifts that appear to be

given for the purpose not only of meeting a need of the moment but also for validating the message of Christianity to those who have not heard or believed.

FOR FURTHER STUDY

Scripture Passages

- Romans 12:3-8
- 1 Corinthians 12:4-11, 28-31
- Ephesians 2:19-22
- Ephesians 4:11-16

FAQ #25

Q **What Is the Durative Position?**

A **The Durative position is the belief that the signs and wonders in the New Testament have continued throughout church history and still exist today.**

This is the position held by a large percentage of Pentecostal, charismatic, and third wave believers. Before we look more closely at the position, however, it might be helpful to understand these twenti-

Perception of ideas rather than the storing of them should be the aim of education. The mind should be an eye to see with rather than a bin to store facts in. The man who has been taught by the Holy Spirit will be a seer rather than a scholar. The difference is that the scholar sees and the seer sees through; and that is a mighty difference indeed.

A. W. Tozer (1897-1963)

eth-century terms better. The first wave of signs and wonders came in the Pentecostal movement in the first part of this century, beginning in the United States and spreading to other parts of the world. It emphasized the experience of being baptized in the Holy Spirit, accompanied by speaking in tongues. Signs and wonders were seen to naturally accompany preaching and belief in this full experience of the gospel. Because Pentecostalism was largely rejected by the established churches, Pentecostal believers organized their own churches. Most of the supernormal activity of the first wave thus took place within Pentecostal churches or circles.

The second wave came in the charismatic renewal of the middle part of the century. Unlike the first wave, the charismatic movement spilled over into the major denominations, including the Catholic Church. This wave too focused on the baptism of the Holy Spirit, which again usually included speaking in tongues. Charismatics emphasized "all" the gifts of the Spirit operating and getting everyone functioning in the body of Christ according to his or her gift. The term "charismatic" was taken from the Greek word for gifts, *charismata*. Charismatics also emphasized exuberant worship, compassion for those in need, and warm, interpersonal relationships—things that many felt often to be missing in noncharismatic circles.

The third wave is a more recent phenomenon, beginning in the 1980s. While third wave believers applaud the work of the Holy Spirit they see in the first two waves, they choose not to be identified with either. Third wave renewal emphasizes miracles, physical healing, demonic exorcisms, and emotional healing. It tends to hold to the classic evangelical view that baptism in the Spirit occurs at conversion and to a role for speaking in tongues that is relatively minor, compared to the first two waves. Many third wavers prefer a less enthusiastic form of worship and are frequently content in traditional evangelical worship services.

Pentecostals, charismatics, and third wave believers generally hold to a Durative perspective on sign gifts. They believe the miraculous spiritual gifts and the signs and wonders that occurred in the New Testament still occur today, as they have to one degree or another since New Testament times. For this reason, we will, for our purposes, lump the varied Pentecostal, charismatic, and third wave positions under the umbrella of the "signs and wonders movement."

These signs and wonders, according to this position, include the following common manifestations of the Spirit:

Tongues: Modern tongues include the miraculous, but infrequent, speaking of an unknown foreign language so that the hearer hears God praised in his or her own language, as we see happening in the second chapter of the Book of Acts. More commonly, tongues occur as the speaking of an unknown prayer language that is either to be spoken in private or, if in public, to be interpreted by someone with the gift of interpretation, as we see in 1 Corinthians 14.

Interpretation: This gift enables one to interpret the foreign or unknown language that someone else is speaking. It is not understood to be a close, word-for-word translation, but an adequate interpretation of the utterance.

Healings: This gift is the actual healing of physical disease, illness, or malady. Some view the gift also as in some sense residing with persons given this gift, with the result that when they pray in faith, those afflicted are frequently healed by God (never by the person with the gift).

Prophecy: This gift refers to a divinely inspired proclamation of God's will, usually for a specific situation. It may but does not have to include the element of prediction, and it is never viewed as having the authority to supplant or override God's written word.

Exorcism: This gift consists both of the Spirit-given ability to discern the influence of demonic spirits and to effectively command them to leave individuals under their influence.

Evaluation

Some, of course, see major problems with this position. Among them are (1) the biblical violations and excesses of the signs and wonders movement; (2) the fact that, to many, the gifts in the New Testament seem much more predictable, effective, dramatic, and verifiable than today; and (3) biblical and historical support for the view that the signs and wonders recorded in the New Testament may have existed for a specific purpose, and when that purpose passed, the signs and wonders themselves passed.

FAQ #26

 What Is the Cessationist Position?

 The Cessationist position states that New Testament signs and wonders disappeared with the passing of the apostles and the establishment of the Scriptures and are not intended ever to reappear again.

The Cessationist position, generally, holds the following views:
Tongues: Modern tongues are a psychological phenomenon at best and demonic at worst. Glossolalia (speaking in tongues) is not confined to Pentecostal, charismatic, or third wave movements. It is found among Eskimos, Eastern religions, New Agers, those in mental institutions, and occultists. This is not to say that Christians fall into any of these categories. It is merely to say that tongues by themselves are not a sign of anything. Apparently, a certain percentage of people have the innate capacity to speak in tongues, and some do so in Christian contexts. It does not, however, constitute a duplication of the New Testament gift.

Interpretations: Since biblical tongues do not exist, there is no need for the gift of interpretation either.

Healings: God does heal miraculously today. However, the healings that are seen in charismatic circles today occur in answer to prayer, by God's sovereign decision to heal, or as a result of powerful psychological forces that can affect healing. The New Testament gift of healing does not exist.

Prophecy: The ability to tell the future or to speak directly for God is a gift that passed with the apostles and New Testament prophets and does not exist today.

Exorcisms: No gift of discerning spirits or exorcism exists today. The Epistles tell us to have our spiritual armor in place and stand firm (Ephesians 6:10-18), and to resist the devil and he will flee from us (James 4:7).

Evaluation

There are problems with a rigid Cessationist position also. First, nowhere in the Bible are signs and wonders and miraculous gifts of the Spirit explicitly said to have ceased, never to reappear again. Add to that the fact that many bright young Pentecostal, charismatic, and third wave scholars are amassing better biblical support for the validity of their positions—and answering objections to their position— than they have ever done before. Their diligent scholarship has made the standard Cessationist arguments more vulnerable. In addition, strict Cessationists who allow for little or no miraculous activity today must find a way to explain many rather amazing things that are reported by sound, mature Christians.

For example, I have friends ministering in primitive areas who tell stories of unbelievable things. These are people whom I respect in every other way, but they have these outrageous stories to tell, often relating to demonic activity.

My wife and I also have a close friend who is a woman of unusual wisdom, maturity, and insight. She has sacrificed most modern comforts for a life of hardship and deprivation as a missionary. Yet

Unless I understand what the Bible teaches about signs and wonders, I may fall prey to an illicit use of them, or, on the other hand, I may discount something that is actually a work of God. I neither want to be deluded into believing in something that is not of God, nor to miss out on what God is doing in His world.

she is only really happy when she is on the mission field. She is a lady of grace, humility, and solid biblical knowledge. She is not a Pentecostal or a charismatic, and she has nothing in her past to predispose her toward anything sensational. Yet when she talks of what has happened to her, to Christian friends of hers, or to other people she knows, your jaw goes slack and the hair at the back of your neck prickles. She tells stories of what could be called "power encounters" and "power evangelism," because there are signs and wonders that surround her life and ministry.

Some sincere Christians say "Yes!" some say "Never!" and some say "Perhaps."

It is common to hear reports from missionaries and read stories of missionaries in primitive parts of Africa, Asia, the Philippines, and other places, telling stories of visible angels surrounding and protecting missionary housing, of Elijah-like fire erupting spontaneously on ceremonial altars to prove which god was the true God, or of miraculous healings. The people who tell these stories are bright people, people of integrity, people of biblical knowledge and spiritual maturity. They are people who appear normal in every respect except one: Their lives are interwoven with miraculous events.

Similar stories increasingly are being told by people in inner city ghettos, in wealthy suburbs where Satan worship and the occult are growing at an alarming rate, and in more modern countries (as opposed to Third World countries), such as Russia and China, where Christianity had been "officially" stamped out.

What do you do with such people? You can look them squarely in the eyes and call them bold-faced liars. You can listen politely, and then afterwards tell your spouse what a pity it is that they have one corner flapping in the wind. You can believe they are deluded, tricked, or having regular bad dreams. Or you can accept what they are saying as true, and then go back to the Bible to see if you can "square" it with

Scripture. Non-Pentecostal/charismatics/third wavers do so, some-times, by advancing what some have called an "Approximation" position.

FAQ #27

What Is the Approximation Position?

The Approximation position holds that the miraculous gifts and signs and wonders are not fully operative today, but that a reduced form of the gifts operates today under the apparent blessing of God.

The "Durative" view and the "Cessationist" view both can be presented rather easily because they paint the issues in black and white. One says that the full New Testament miraculous gifts and signs and wonders are in existence today, and the other says they aren't. Positions other than these two usually take careful, more thorough explanation. While variations of this position are espoused by many, one version has been well articulated by James Packer in his book *Keep in Step with the Spirit* (especially chapter 6).

He makes the point that if you apply two key biblical criteria to the modern signs and wonders movement, you have a measure of its validity. First is a doctrinal test: "Do they declare that Jesus is Lord?" (1 John 2:22; 4:1-3). Second is a moral test: "Do they manifest love for God by keeping His commandments, striving to avoid sin and loving their brethren in Christ?" (1 John 2:4; 3:9-10, 17, 24; 4:7-13, 20-21; 5:1-3). By these two tests, he asserts, the modern charismatic movement, as a whole, passes the tests (Packer, p. 185).

He goes on to state that "most Protestant charismatics outside Germany embrace...the restorationist view," making the essence of the disciples' experience on the Day of Pentecost, as described in Acts 2, and of the Corinthians' experience, as described in 1 Corinthians 12-14, into norms, ideals, and goals for Christians now. (The difference between the Durative view [my term] and the Restorationist view [Packer's term] is that the Durative view holds that the gifts never disappeared. The Restorationist view holds that they did disappear in the centuries following Christ, but have been restored today.)

Healing in the New Testament was successful, instantaneous, and permanent..

In what he calls a "retheologized view," Packer argues that the miraculous gifts and the signs and wonders of the New Testament are not convincingly in operation today, but that an approximation of the gifts is, with God's apparent blessing—hence the name "Approximation" view. This view, as explained by Packer, holds these positions on the following issues:

Tongues: Modern tongues are not the supernatural ability to speak foreign languages as they were in the Bible, but are essentially a spiritual/psychological phenomenon that, like any meaningful spiritual experience, may help a person live a more satisfying and fruitful life. Charismatic glossolalia (speaking in tongues), which is frequently a learned skill and technique, lacks language structure, and its own practitioners regard it as mainly for private use. It cannot be convincingly equated with the tongues of 1 Corinthians 12-14, which were for public use, served as a sign to unbelievers, and which Paul apparently considered a language conveying meaning and therefore capable of being interpreted. Even though it is not a restoration of a New Testament gift, God is using glossolalia today to enrich people's personal spiritual lives. It is subject to misuse and disappointment for some, but that does not discount its positive benefit to others if we are to take abundant personal testimony at face value.

Interpretation: If modern tongues are not a restoration of the New Testament gift, then modern interpretation is the least credible of all modern charismatic manifestations. Packer suggests that "interpretations prove to be as stereotyped, vague, and uninformative as they are spontaneous, fluent, and confident."

Healings: Jesus and the apostles healed directly with their word or their touch, healing was instantaneous, and they healed in very large numbers. On occasion they raised individuals who had been dead for days. There is no record that they ever attempted to heal without success (except in the one case of demon possession where the disciples failed to pray and Jesus had to take over [Mark 9:17-29]), and no one who was healed relapsed soon after. Whatever else can be said of modern faith healers, none of them has a track record like this.

Several things must be said under "healings," however. First, it must be admitted that God does appear to be healing miraculously today. Sometimes it is spontaneous, sometimes as a result of prayer, and sometimes it follows a laying on of hands. We cannot discount God's prerogative to heal diseases and physical maladies today. What is in question is the "gift" of healing. If someone had the gift of healing today on the scale that existed in the New Testament, there would be no question about it. "The most we can say of charismatic healers is that at some moments and in some respects they are enabled to perform like the gifted healers of New Testament times, and every such occasion confirms that God's touch still has its ancient power. But that is much less than saying that in the ministry of these folk the New Testament gift of healing reappears" (Packer, p. 214).

Prophecy: New Testament prophecy was twofold. First, prophets spoke forth the word of God in power. Second, some prophets some of the time were able to tell the future, or give direct revelation from God. Looking only at the first characteristic, we have prophets today in the New Testament sense. But if you include telling the future or giving direct revelation, then the gift of prophecy does not exist as a restoration of the New Testament gift. Being able to speak confidently like Jeremiah, with the statement, "Thus sayeth the Lord," is not convincingly established in the charismatic movement.

> **G**od is working to renew Christ's image in each believer.

Exorcisms: Packer does not address the issue of exorcisms.

In summary, according to Packer's view, it cannot be convincingly concluded that the New Testament gifts have, after a period of dormancy, been given back to the church just as they were. Nor can it be convincingly concluded that the gifts have endured since New Testament times and are revived to New Testament levels. Neither of these views is supported from Scripture or experience. If we want to discern what God may be doing in the Pentecostal, charismatic, and third wave movements, we must think about it in other terms. We must explain what is going on in some way other than to say that the New Testament miraculous gifts are fully restored.

Godly and credible people hold divergent views.

If they are not the restored gifts, what are they? Packer asserts that the newer charismatic movement at the leadership level is less dogmatic about issues such as a distinctive view of baptism of the Holy Spirit, speaking in tongues, and so forth, viewing them not so much as hard requirements for salvation or a mature Christian life, but increasingly as sanctified natural abilities (Packer, p. 221). As such, he views what God is doing among charismatics today as being "essentially what he is doing in the lives of all believing, regenerate people everywhere—namely, working to renew Christ's image in each, so that trust, love, hope, patience, commitment, loyalty, self-denial and self-giving, obedience and joy, may increasingly be seen in us" (Packer, p. 222).

Variations

There are variations on the "Approximation" position, and it is important to understand that those who do not experience or practice miraculous gifts do not have a unified position on them or have just one way to explain some of the more unusual things that sometimes happen. It is a struggle for many believers to reconcile, as much as is possible, the apparently contradictory claims made by otherwise godly and credible people on both sides of the "signs and wonders" issue.

Two variations on the "Approximation" position are the "Sovereignty" view and the "Duplication" view.

These two views are essentially within the Approximation camp, but have different elements and emphases.

The Sovereignty view distinguishes between miraculous gifts and God's sovereign choice to act and perform miracles. This position emphasizes that God is certainly working miracles today. He is healing and doing other extraordinary things, but He is doing them through His sovereign choice, not through people possessing miraculous spiritual gifts. Sometimes He acts in response to prayer and extraordinary faith, but other times He simply chooses when and what miracle He will perform.

According to this view, the presence of a spiritual gift would manifest itself in a highly consistent success rate, like those with the gift of healing in the New Testament. It is true that there are instances in the New Testament when a gifted person was unsuccessful. For example, even Jesus, when He returned to His hometown of Nazareth, "did not do many miracles there because of their unbelief" (Matthew 13:58). And it is also true that a person who is not gifted might see miracles in his ministry. Nevertheless, the issue is consistency. The possession of a gift would offer a much higher degree of consistency and obvious success than we see today. Certainly, some extraordinary things are going on in the church around the world, but they are being done, according to this view, not through individuals who have miraculous gifts, but through the sovereign action of God. When this sovereign action of God occurs frequently in the ministry of some individuals, it may give the appearance that the individual through whom God is working has a miraculous gift.

The second view, the Duplication view, holds that miraculous gifts and signs and wonders had a primary lasting purpose of validating the new message of salvation by grace through faith in Christ (Hebrews 2:3-4) and that whenever the circumstances that called for the original miraculous gifts and signs and wonders are duplicated, the miraculous gifts and signs and wonders could reappear. In the same vein, if the circumstances that called for the original signs and wonders are approximated but not

> The early church faced a hostile, unbelieving environment.

duplicated, you would see an approximation of the signs and wonders but not a duplication, which makes it, in that case, virtually identical to the Approximation view. The Duplication view differs from the Approximation view by holding out the possibility of a full reinstatement of miraculous gifts and signs and wonders if there is a full duplication of the circumstances that called for them originally. The difference is largely a matter of degree.

It might be helpful to clarify what is meant by "a duplication of the circumstances that called for the original gifts." The original circumstances were that a new message of salvation was being proclaimed to people who had never heard it before. Christianity was not established, the Bible was not recognized, there was much resistance to the new message by established religious leaders who were against any new religion, and there was demonic resistance. If these circumstances reappeared, there might be a reappearance of the miraculous gifts, according to this view.

Let us suppose, for example, that a missionary makes contact with people in the heart of the rain forest in the Philippines. These people have never seen a Caucasian before; they know nothing of electricity or aviation or world politics or anything of the modern world. They are completely cut off from modern life. They have never heard the name of God, they have never heard of Jesus, and not only have they never heard of the Bible, they can't even read. Their language has never been reduced to writing. They are entirely ignorant of anything that might predispose them to believe in Christianity.

They are, however, very religious. They worship a spirit that they believe inhabits a huge tree. Every day, one of the villagers must sacrifice a chicken on a rock at the base of the tree, and once a year, on the new year, they must sacrifice a pig. If they don't, they are convinced that terrible things will happen to them. Their sacrifice is a distinct hardship on them, because it is expensive. That's 364 chickens and one pig a year taken out of their village economy. They need those animals to feed themselves, yet they sacrifice them to the "cause" so that something worse will not happen to them.

In this context, along comes a missionary who says, "You don't have to sacrifice these animals to the tree god any more. Jesus is more powerful than the tree god, and He will keep you safe." The villagers eye the missionary suspiciously. They would like to believe him, but do they dare? What if the missionary is wrong? What if this new God, whom they have never heard of, know nothing about, and have seen no evidence of, is not stronger than the tree god? What if the missionary, who has very little credibility with them because he is an outsider, is wrong? There is no way of knowing if his word can be trusted. The missionary has never felt the wrath of the tree god.

This situation would be, in principle, a duplication of the environment that called for the sign gifts in the Bible. If miraculous gifts and signs and wonders accompanied the new message, it would give the villagers a foundation for belief. They would be believing "something" rather than "nothing," just as in the New Testament story.

Evaluation

This position has its problems, too. Much of the Approximation view is built on arguments from silence. It takes the silence of Scripture and begins making conceivable arguments of probability that are then read back into Scripture. For example, the statement, "There is nothing in the Bible that explicitly states that the miraculous gifts and signs and wonders cannot re-emerge if the circumstances that called for them originally are duplicated," is true; but it also rests on what the Bible does not say, not on what it does say.

THINKING BACK

We see, then, that no matter what position you take on this matter, there are problems with it. Unfortunately, we do not have the option of an airtight view held by all evangelical believers. Whatever position we take, therefore, it must accommodate what the Bible teaches, and it must integrate the experiences of mature believers, and it must accommodate the Scriptural injunction to "preserve the unity of the Spirit in the bond of peace" (Ephesians 4:3 NASB).

Though each side of the signs and wonders issue has its strengths and weaknesses, each side seems fully prepared to champion its strengths and defend its weaknesses to the other side. The "signs and wonders" people sometimes look at the others and say that they are straight as a gun barrel theologically and just as empty spiritually. The "no signs and wonders" people sometimes look at the others and say that they have put their minds in their hip pockets and are reading subjective experiences back into the biblical text.

By a fuller understanding of the issues, we might be able to experience greater legitimate unity in the future. If we can hold each other's spiritual and intellectual integrity in greater respect, we might find that our position (whatever it happens to be) might not be the only possible interpretation, and we can find greater unity than if we take our conclusions, press them to the extreme, and attack one another as enemies. This is not to say that it is wrong to disagree with others on biblical interpretation. That is inevitable. But if we earnestly try, we might find more things on which we agree, fewer things about which we must be dogmatic, and present our convictions in a way that upholds the integrity of others, rather than attacking those with whom we do not agree.

Spiritual name-calling does not advance the gospel.

With such great enemies outside the church, we can hardly afford the luxury of infighting over things for which there is room for responsible and enlightened disagreement. If it is a matter that affects salvation or the integrity of Scripture, or another doctrine on which we cannot get "soft" without endangering the integrity of the Christian message, then we dare not compromise. But if well-meaning, spiritually mature, well-educated Christians who agree on the essentials of the Christian faith happen to disagree on matters within that over-all unity, then we can search for greater understanding and unity. Whether it is the issues between Calvinists and Arminians, dispensationalists and the Reformed, or charismatic or non-charismatic, these points of contention often divide people who are clearly Christian. On these matters, we would do well to "endeavor to keep the unity of the Spirit in the bond of peace" (Ephesians 4:3).

Outside the gate are camped Islamic fundamentalism, Eastern religions, the New Age movement, secularism and secular humanism, animism, voodoo, Satanism, witchcraft, the occult, materialism, hedonism (the pursuit of pleasure), and an explosion of cults. These oppose the gospel itself, not merely an interpretation of a few dimensions of the Christian life and ministry. In our disputes within the faith, we are sometimes like soldiers in the trenches, swatting each other for stepping on our spit-polished shoes, while the invading hordes are cresting the nearest hill. It is an old saying, but still true: "In essentials, unity; in nonessentials, diversity; in all things, charity."

SPEED BUMP!

Slow down long enough to be sure you've gotten the main points of this section.

1. **What is the Durative position?**
The Durative position is the belief that the signs and wonders in the New Testament have continued throughout church history and still exist today.

2. **What is the Cessationist position?**
The Cessationist position states that New Testament signs and wonders disappeared with the passing of the apostles and the establishment of the Scriptures and are not intended ever to reappear again.

3. **What is the Approximation position?**
The Approximation position holds that the miraculous gifts and signs and wonders are not fully operative today, but that a reduced form of the gifts operates today under the apparent blessing of God.

FOR FURTHER STUDY

Scripture Passages

- John 17:20-23
- Romans 12:4-8
- 1 Corinthians 12:4-8
- 1 Corinthians 12:23-27
- Ephesians 4:1-16

FAQ #28

Q What Is the Pentecostal/Charismatic Interpretation of Ephesians 5:18?

A The Pentecostal/charismatic interpretation is that the filling of the Spirit here neither requires nor rules out supernormal experiences such as speaking in tongues.

Charismatics (and with them Pentecostal and third wave Christians) believe that Spirit-fillings of the type common in Acts occur today as well, complete with supernormal experiences such as speaking in tongues. Regarding Ephesians 5:18, however, they agree that speaking in tongues and other high-profile manifestations of the Spirit are not mentioned and are not a necessary result of the ongoing infilling of the Spirit, but neither are they ruled out. The term "fullness" is a favorite both in Ephesians (1:10, 23; 3:19; 4:13) and to charismatic believers, and they would urge all believers to yield to the ongoing filling of the Spirit in their lifelong seeking to "be filled with all the fullness of God" (Ephesians 3:19).

Charismatics stress that Ephesians 5:18 should be read keeping in mind all that Acts records about the ministry of the gospel in Ephesus, perhaps only a few years earlier (Acts 19-20). They believe that the context provided by Acts alerts us to ways that Ephesians 5:18-21 may point to "charismatic" activity as a part of the

> "The Holy Spirit expects us to take seriously the answers he has already provided, the light he has already shed; and he does not expect us to plead for things that have already been denied."
>
> *Paul Little*

filling of the Spirit here. For example, the close connection between being "filled with the Spirit" (v. 18) and "spiritual songs" invites reference to the charismatic singing described in 1 Corinthians 14:15-16, 26.

In any event, charismatics point out that one consistent result of any Spirit filling is some form of Spirit-inspired speech—whether tongues or prophecy (Acts 2:4; 4:31; 19:6), or "speaking to one another in psalms and hymns and spiritual songs" (Ephesians 5:19). Another result is well-being within the body of Christ—whether the creation of a wholly new community of faith as on the day of Pentecost (Acts 2:46-47), or Christlike service, "submitting to one another in the fear of God" as Ephesians 5:21 directs.

The charismatic view, then, would be that the filling of the Spirit in view in Ephesians 5:18 results in Spirit-inspired speech (often worship) and service within the body of Christ. It neither requires nor rules out specifically "charismatic" manifestations such as tongues.

FAQ #29

Q What Is the "Victorious Christian Life" Interpretation of Ephesians 5:18?

A The "victorious Christian life" interpretation is that the filling of the Spirit empowers a person for improved Christian living and greater ministry.

A second major interpretation is that of the "victorious Christian life." This position maintains that the filling of the Spirit is God's empowering for victorious Christian living and service. It does not result in any miraculous manifestations such as speaking in tongues and prophesying. But it does result in greater power for deliverance from sin, for living a Christian lifestyle, and for ministry.

Certain conditions must be met, according to this tradition, in order to be filled; and when these conditions are met, believers are then filled with the Spirit. This filling must be taken by faith, since there are often no immediate observable results. These conditions vary slightly according to different Bible teachers, but usually include the following:

1. Dedicating one's life to the Lord in an initial, crisis-like act in which one gives his life to God for His will to be done through it (Charles Ryrie, *A Survey of Bible Doctrine,* p. 83). This initial dedication must be followed by a lifestyle of continual dedication to the will of God and daily dependence on the Holy Spirit.
2. Confessing sin and putting away any sins that you are harboring in your life;
3. Asking to be filled; and
4. Believing that God did, indeed, fill with His Spirit, even though one may see or feel no evidence of it.

Why Do I Need to Know What It Means to Be Filled with the Holy Spirit?

1. I need to know so I can experience all that Jesus wants me to experience in my walk with Him.
2. I need to know so I will not expect something from God that He does not intend to give me.
3. I need to know so I will not take on a burden that God does not intend for me to carry.
4. I need to know so I can explain the truth to others.

FAQ #30

 What Is the "Word of Christ" Interpretation of Ephesians 5:18?

 The "word of Christ" interpretation is that the filling of the Spirit is essentially the same as "letting the word of Christ dwell in you richly."

According to this view, the results of being filled with the Spirit in Ephesians 5:18 are the same as the results of "letting the word of Christ dwell in you richly" in Colossians 3:16. Therefore, since the consequences are the same, they are seen as essentially the same thing.

In Ephesians 5:19-6:6 the results of being filled with the Spirit are

- speaking in psalms,
- singing,
- giving thanks,
- and a harmony of relationships between husbands and wives, parents and children, masters and slaves.

In Colossians 3:16-22 we see the same results:

- teaching with psalms,
- singing,
- thankfulness,
- and harmony between husbands and wives, parents and children, masters and slaves.

The results in Colossians are produced, however, not by being filled with the Spirit, but by "let[ting] the word of Christ dwell in you richly." Being filled with the Spirit and letting the word of Christ dwell in you produce exactly the same results. Therefore, careful attention must be paid to the possible link between the two.

The "word of Christ" in Colossians 3:16 does not refer explicitly to the New Testament, because the New Testament had not all been written yet. It refers, however, to that which was known to the Colossians about Jesus and His teachings, even though the New Testament was not yet complete. By implication, today it would apply to the entire Bible, with a special emphasis on the central place Christ's ministry and teachings hold.

To allow the word of Christ to dwell within us, we must read the word of God, study it, memorize it, and meditate on it, with a spirit of obedience. As we do, the Holy Spirit illumines the truth of the Scripture to us (1 Corinthians 2:9-16); convicts us of sin (John 16:8); strengthens us for righteous living and worship (Ephesians 3:14-21); and nurtures His fruit within us so that we experience love, joy, peace, longsuffering, kindness, goodness, faithfulness, gentleness, and self-control (Galatians 5:22-23). As this process begins, grows, and bears fruit, we are filled with the Spirit.

FAQ #31

Q **What Happens When We are Filled With the Spirit?**

A **There are four primary results: we involve ourselves in mutual ministry to others, we experience inner joy, we cultivate an attitude of gratitude, and we live in a spirit of mutual submission to others.**

While all three of the above traditions might not agree on all the possible conditions for being filled with the Spirit or all the possible results, they do agree on the ones listed in the Ephesians 5 passage. The consequence of the Spirit-filled life is a heart that desires to minister to others, a heart that experiences joy, a heart that is grateful, and a heart that serves.

Mutual Ministry

Speaking to one another in psalms and hymns and spiritual songs.
Ephesians 5:19

Christians are not to be rugged individualists, standing alone, or as islands unto themselves. Nor are we to erect barriers between ourselves and others, daring them to cross. As part of the body of Christ, we need others, and others need us.

Each of us has been gifted to minister to others, and we are responsible to exercise that gift. Some of us, of course, have been called by God to labor vocationally in ministry. But God intends for all of us to minister when opportunity arises—in our workplaces, in our neighborhoods, in our families, and in our society. Realizing that we have this personal responsibility and then having a heart to help others is a mark of being filled with the Holy Spirit.

God intends for each believer to minister to others.

The totality of all believers—all true Christians—is called the body of Christ. The human body is a picture of that spiritual body. By observing how the human body functions, we gain insight into how the spiritual body should function.

For example, consider the cooperation of the entire body involved when a toddler takes his first steps:

If we traced all the body signals involved in walking, we would find in that grinning, perilously balanced toddler a machine of unfathomable complexity. Over one hundred million sense cells in each eye compose a picture of the table he is walking toward. Stretch receptors in the neck relate the attitude of his head to the trunk and maintain appropriate muscle tension. Joint receptors fire off messages that report the angles of limb bones. The sense organs inside the ear inform the brain of the

> direction of gravity and the body's balance. Pressure from the
> ground on each toe triggers messages about the type of surface
> on which he is walking...A casual glance down to avoid a toy on
> the carpet will cause all these sense organs to shift dramatically;
> the image of the ground moves rapidly across the retina, but the
> inner ear and stretch receptors assure the brain the body is not
> falling. Any movement of the head alters the body's center of
> gravity, affecting the tension in each of the limb muscles. The
> toddler's body crackles with millions of messages informing his
> brain and giving directions to perform the extraordinary feat of
> walking (Paul Brand and Philip Yancey, *Fearfully and
> Wonderfully Made*).

When seen up close, in detail, the physical act of walking is a
stupefying miracle. When seen up close, in detail, the spiritual act of
"walking together" is an equally stupefying miracle. It requires millions of individual beings, contaminated by the impulse to act inde-
pendently, to reject that impulse and subordinate themselves to the
leading of Jesus, the Head, and move in concert with His will rather
than millions of individual wills. The miracle of spiritual unity is no
less awesome than the miracle of physical unity.

Lone rangers are not filled with the Spirit. Human islands are not
filled with the Spirit. Human porcupines are not filled with the Holy
Spirit.

Those who are filled with the Holy Spirit sense the importance of
mutual ministry. They understand that they are part of a larger whole,
and they see the need for unity with the Head and the body of which
they are a part.

Out of that sense of wholeness the Spirit-filled life finds joy.

Inner Joy

Singing and making melody in your heart to the Lord.
> **Ephesians 5:19**

You need not have a beautiful voice to have a beautiful heart. Yet
when the Holy Spirit invades your heart, inner joy expresses itself in
inner song. And this inner joy does not depend on circumstances. It
survives in spite of circumstances.

In his book *Winning over Pain, Fear and Worry*, John Haggai tells how his son suffered severe physical trauma at birth because the doctor, a respected obstetrician, was intoxicated at the time.

During the first year of the little lad's life, eight doctors said he could not possibly survive. For the first two years of his life, my wife had to feed him every three hours with a Brecht feeder. It took a half hour to prepare for the feeding and it took another half hour to clean up and put him back to bed. Not once during that time did she ever get out of the house for any diversion whatsoever. Never did she get more than two hours sleep at one time.

My wife, Christine, had once been acclaimed by some of the nation's leading musicians as one of the outstanding contemporary female vocalists in America. From the time she was thirteen she had been popular as a singer—and constantly in the public eye. Hers was the experience of receiving and rejecting some fancy offers with even fancier incomes to marry an aspiring Baptist pastor with no church to pastor!

Then, after five years of marriage, the tragedy struck!...She was now marooned within the walls of our home. Her beautiful voice no longer enraptured public audiences (p. 414).

Although John Edmund, Jr., was paralyzed, able to sit in his wheelchair only with the assistance of full-length body braces, his parents rejoiced to have him with them for over twenty years—and rejoiced that he committed his heart and life to Jesus Christ and evidenced genuine concern for the things of the Lord.

I attribute his commitment to Jesus Christ and his wonderful dis-
position to the sparkling radiance of an emotionally mature,
Christ-centered mother who has mastered the discipline of living
one day at a time. Never have I—nor has anyone else—heard a
word of complaint from her (p. 415).

Ah, God's mercy. Sometimes it is so severe. Yet the Spirit-filled life
is a life of joy, surviving not because of the circumstances, but in spite
of them.

I believe that some people, like Christine Haggai, are gifted to
respond to music more than others. But everyone who is filled with
the Spirit will enjoy and appreciate the music of the soul that lifts his
or her heart to God.

And out of that joy the Spirit-filled heart gives thanks.

Gratitude

Giving thanks always for all things to God the Father in the name of
our Lord Jesus Christ.
Ephesians 5:20

When we trace the word "thanksgiving" through the Bible—both
the Old and New Testaments—we get a sense of God's attitude toward
gratitude. Consider just a few passages:

For in the days of David and Asaph, in ancient times, there were
leaders of the singers, songs of praise and hymns of thanksgiving to God.
Nehemiah 12:46 (NASB)

**I will praise the name of God with song, and shall magnify Him
with thanksgiving.**
Psalm 69:30 (NASB)

**Let us come before His presence with thanksgiving; Let us
shout joyfully to Him with psalms.**
Psalm 95:2

**Enter into His gates with thanksgiving, And into His courts with
praise. Be thankful to Him, and bless His name.**
Psalm 100:4

**Blessing and glory and wisdom, thanksgiving and honor and
power and might, be to our God forever and ever. Amen.**
Revelation 7:12

With this kind of emphasis, it is little wonder that the third manifestation of the filling of the Holy Spirit is a grateful heart. Having
20/20 spiritual sight, the Spirit-filled heart is thankful.

If we understood how perilously our lives hang in the balance
as we go about our daily routine, if we understood how vigorous the
spiritual warfare is around us, if we understood how fortunate we are
to have food on the table, a roof over our heads, and clothes on our
backs, if we grasped how dependent we are on the common grace of
God and the goodness of others for our basic necessities in life, we
would be grateful people. We would be grateful for what we do have,
rather than ungrateful for what we do not have. If we truly grasped
our sin, and that it is because of the Lord's mercies that we are not
consumed (Lamentations 3:22), yes, we would be more grateful.

Finally, the heart that ministers to others, beating with joy and
thanksgiving, is truly the heart of a servant.

A Servant Heart
Submitting to one another in the fear of God.
Ephesians 5:21

Anyone who knows anything about chickens knows that there is
a pecking order in the barnyard. There is a Top Chicken, who can

peck any other chicken in the barnyard without fear of reprisal. And there is a Bottom Chicken, who can't peck anybody without fear of reprisal. All the other chickens are aligned in a hierarchy of power between these two.

Power struggles are not consistent with Christ's kingdom.

If a kernel of corn falls between any two chickens, the one with a higher pecking order gets the kernel. If there is any question as to which is which, a fracas breaks out—anywhere from a skirmish to all-out war. When the fight is over, the winner establishes or reestablishes dominance over the other, and the hierarchy adjusts itself accordingly from top to bottom.

The same order can be observed in the great chicken coop of life. In the various coops we frequent (job, school, church, neighborhood, etc.) there are top humans and bottom humans, and all in between are aligned in a hierarchy of power—a great human pecking order.

If an opportunity for advancement falls between two humans, a fracas breaks out—anywhere from a little skirmish to all-out war. This can mean anything from dirty looks to murder, whereby humans establish dominance over other humans, and the hierarchy is established.

Just as chickens constantly jockey for position in the barnyard pecking order, so humans constantly jockey for power in the chicken coop of life. It is only natural. As Christians, however, we are not to participate in this great posturing for position. We are not to act naturally; we are to act supernaturally.

A case in point occurred when James and John, two brothers who were Christ's disciples, began jockeying for position in the coming kingdom (Mark 10:35-45). "Master," they said, "when your kingdom comes, let one of us sit on your right hand and the other on your left." They wanted to be top chickens in the kingdom of God.

"Men, you have it all wrong," Jesus replied. "That's the way the world acts. They love to lord it over others. But things are entirely different in My kingdom. In My kingdom, if you want to be great, you must become a servant to everyone else."

What a shock! In heaven, the pecking order is reversed. The first shall be last and the last shall be first. Those who humble themselves, God exalts. Those who exalt themselves, God humbles.

"For even the Son of Man did not come to be served, but to serve, and to give His life a ransom for many (Mark 10:45).

THINKING BACK

Corrie ten Boom, a Dutch Christian who was imprisoned in a German concentration camp during World War II for helping and hiding Jews in the Netherlands, wrote in her marvelous book, *Tramp for the Lord*:

The war was over. Even before I left the concentration camp, I knew I would be busy helping those who had lost their way. Now I found myself starting just such a work in Bloemendaal (Holland). It was more than a home for the homeless; it was a refuge for those who had lost their way spiritually as well as physically.

Yet, because I had lived so close to death, looking it in the face day after day, I often felt like a stranger among my own people—many of whom looked upon money, honor of men, and success as the important issues of life. Standing in front of a cre-

matorium, knowing that any day could be your last day, gives one a different perspective on life. The words of an old German motto kept flashing in my mind:

"What I spent, I had; what I saved, I lost; what I gave, I have."

How well I understood the feeling of the artist who painted the picture of the corpse of a once wealthy man and entitled it, *Sic transit gloria mundi*—So passes the glory of this world. The material things of this world no longer excited me—nor would they ever again (p. 29).

Our task is to yield to the Spirit of God.

When we are filled with the Spirit, we get our eyes off this world and onto the Lord.

Though there are differences among Christians in their understandings of what it means to be filled with the Spirit, there are also common beliefs, and there is great value in highlighting these common beliefs. Mature Christians of all three of the above traditions would agree that our task is to yield to the Spirit of God, to worship God in spirit and in truth, and to build up the community He creates by serving one another in the way Christ served all (Philippians 2:1-16).

Christians of all three traditions would agree that we should cultivate an awareness of the presence of the Spirit within us to be alert to His leading, His convicting, His illuminating ministry, and to be ready to follow Him in total obedience. We must be responsive to Him when He moves in our lives in extraordinary ways and leads us to worship the Lord and serve Him with unusual anointing. We must live in relationship to the Holy Spirit and allow Him to have His way in our lives. Whatever the filling of the Holy Spirit means, it must surely include the things that Christians agree on.

SPEED BUMP!

Slow down to be sure you've gotten the main points of this section.

1. What is the Pentecostal/charismatic interpretation of Ephesians 5:18?

The Pentecostal/charismatic interpretation is that the filling of the Spirit here neither requires nor rules out super-normal experiences such as speaking in tongues.

2. What is the "victorious Christian life" interpretation of Ephesians 5:18?

The "victorious Christian life" interpretation is that the filling of the Spirit empowers a person for improved Christian living and greater ministry.

3. What is the "word of Christ" interpretation of Ephesians 5:18?

The "word of Christ" interpretation is that the filling of the Spirit is essentially the same as "letting the word of Christ dwell in you richly."

FOR FURTHER STUDY

Scripture Passages

- Mark 10:42-45
- John 15:7-11
- Acts 2:1-21
- Romans 8:1-17
- Galatians 5:16-23
- Galatians 6:10
- Ephesians 5:17-21
- Colossians 3:16-22
- 1 Thessalonians 5:18

FAQ #32

 Can We Sin So Often that God Will Not Forgive Us?

 We cannot sin so often that God will not forgive us.

The apostle Peter did us a great favor. He flew off the handle. He exaggerated. He lied. He cursed. He chickened out of things. He broke his word. He manipulated. And not just to men, but also to God. He told Jesus he would do things that he didn't do. He told Him that he would stick with Him to the end. He didn't. He ended up hiding in the shadows while Jesus was taken to the cross.

I do not rejoice in Peter's sin. I wish for him that he had not committed those sins. But he did, and in doing so, he taught us something terribly important. All of us have some of Peter's blood flowing in our veins. All of us have lied, broken our word, gotten angry, and denied Jesus, either directly or indirectly. We feel terrible about it—so bad that sometimes we question whether or not we are even true Christians. Or we get so hopelessly frustrated that we give up trying. And we may wonder if there is ever a point where God gives up on us.

In the eighteenth chapter of the Gospel of Matthew, beginning with verse 21, Peter asked Jesus, "How often shall my brother sin against me, and I forgive him? Up to seven times?" My guess is that someone had sinned against Peter several times and he had had it. Perhaps he was looking for an out, a way to deal with this person who had sinned against

> "Sin is like ice in our pipes—our spiritual lives have been 'frozen.' There is only one solution, and that is repentance to clear the blockage and restore the flow of the Holy Spirit."
>
> *Billy Graham*

him more than once. He must have reached for the highest number imaginable to him at the moment. He may even have thought that this number was going to impress Jesus or the other disciples who heard him ask the question. I can even hear him clearing his throat before he gives the Big Number. "How often shall my brother sin against me and I forgive him? Up to (ahem) seven times?"

Think about that. Not to give Peter too hard a time, seven is a lot of times if the seven times occur very close together. Peter was being more gracious and forbearing than a lot of us. How many times do you forgive drivers who cut in front of you in traffic? How many times do you forgive a waiter or waitress who is rude to you? How many times do you forgive a friend or family member who says something unkind to you? In those terms, seven seems like a lot.

> We all are a bit like Peter.

In spite of that, Jesus said, "I do not say to you up to seven times, but up to seventy times seven." I don't think Jesus meant 490 times. Rather, I think He meant "as often as it happens." If that is the standard to which God holds us, would He not also hold to that standard? That is, if God expects us to forgive a person as many times as that person asks us to forgive him, would not God forgive us as many times as we ask Him?

You see, back when I was struggling so hard to be a good Christian and failing so miserably, I was really trying! A two-hour-a-

Why Do I Need to Know This?

I need to know that if I accept Christ's offer of salvation, I cannot commit the unpardonable sin, no matter how badly or how often I sin. God does not want me to sin, but His grace is equal to my sin as long as I am in Christ. If I have not yet accepted Christ's offer of salvation, I still can do so, no matter what my sins are. I can come to Him at any time, and He will not turn me out.

day commitment for prayer and Bible reading is no small commitment when you are taking a full load of courses and playing basketball, too. I did little else but go to class, study, play/practice basketball, pray, read my Bible, and sleep. I realized later that God was pleased with my effort and my desire. He was perfectly willing to forgive my sins. I just wasn't aware of it at the time.

Later, one sentence from one of my seminary professors ministered great healing to me: "Remember, you can't be holy in a hurry." I thought, "Why hadn't someone told me that?" Perhaps someone had, and I just didn't hear it. Then, Psalm 103:8-14 became one of the most valued passages in all the Bible to me:

The LORD is compassionate and gracious,
Slow to anger and abounding in lovingkindness.
He will not always strive {with us};
Nor will He keep {His anger} forever.
He has not dealt with us according to our sins,
Nor rewarded us according to our iniquities.
For as high as the heavens are above the earth,
So great is His lovingkindness toward those who fear Him.
As far as the east is from the west,
So far has He removed our transgressions from us.
Just as a father has compassion on {his} children,
So the LORD has compassion on those who fear
Him.
For He Himself knows our frame;
He is mindful that we are {but} dust (NASB).

Ahh, so the Lord knows that we are but dust. How comforting. Even so, He will remove our transgressions as far from us as the east is from the west (an infinite distance). That is the message I needed to hear, and that is the message that Peter teaches us by living an imperfect life and asking Jesus the right questions. We cannot sin so many times that God will not forgive us.

FAQ #33

 Can We Sin So Badly that God Will Not Forgive Us?

 We cannot sin so badly that God will not forgive Us.

Not only has Peter's life taught us that we cannot sin *so many times* that God will not forgive us, so he has also taught us that we cannot sin *so badly* that God will not forgive us. Many people have the mistaken feeling that they have committed a sin so bad that God cannot or will not forgive them. The sin varies with the one who committed it. Some feel that adultery is unforgivable, yet Jesus forgave an adulteress in the Scripture (John 8:3-11). Some believe that Jesus cannot forgive murder, yet Jesus forgave those who murdered Him ("Father, forgive them, for they do not know what they do," Luke 23:34). Someone might feel that a life of graft and extortion would be unforgivable, yet Jesus forgave Matthew and Zacchaeus of those sins (Matthew 9:9; Luke 19:1-10).

I always imagined that the greatest sin would be cursing God. Here, too, Peter comes to our rescue. Peter cursed and denied that he ever knew Jesus. We read it in Matthew 26:69-74:

> Now Peter was sitting outside in the courtyard, and a certain servant-girl came to him and said, "You too were with Jesus the Galilean."
> But he denied it before them all, saying, "I do not know

what you are talking about."

And when he had gone out to the gateway, another servant-girl saw him and said to those who were there, "This man was with Jesus of Nazareth."

And again he denied it with an oath, "I do not know the man."

And a little later the bystanders came up and said to Peter, "Surely you too are one of them; for the way you talk gives you away."

Then he began to curse and swear, "I do not know the man!" And immediately a cock crowed (NASB).

The passage does not specifically say that he cursed God, but I have always imagined that he did, for when he denied he ever knew Him, it was with an oath, cursing and swearing. In any event, it seems to me to be the worst thing you could ever do.

As we read on in the account, however, we know that Peter was forgiven, for not many days later we see him eating fish with Jesus on the shore of the Sea of Galilee, in fellowship with Him. Peter demonstrated that we cannot sin so badly but that God will forgive us. I'm sorry, Peter, for your struggles. But I'm grateful for the overall message of your life.

FAQ #34

 What Is the Unpardonable Sin?

 The unpardonable sin is rejecting the Holy Spirit's pull to bring us to Christ.

After saying that we cannot sin so many times but that God will forgive us, and that we cannot sin so badly but that God will forgive us, now we run headlong into what seems to be a contradiction: the unpardonable sin. The Bible does say that there is an unpardonable sin. So, what is it, and how do we reconcile it with what we have already said?

Let's read the passage in Matthew 12:22-32:

> Then there was brought to Him a demon-possessed man who was blind and dumb, and He healed him, so that the dumb man spoke and saw. And all the multitudes were amazed, and began to say, "This man cannot be the Son of David, can he?"
>
> But when the Pharisees heard it, they said, "This man casts out demons only by Beelzebub the ruler of the demons."
>
> And knowing their thoughts He said to them, "Any kingdom divided against itself is laid waste; and any city or house divided against itself shall not stand. And if Satan casts out Satan, he is divided against himself; how then shall his kingdom stand?
>
> "And if I by Beelzebub cast out demons, by whom do your sons cast them out? Consequently they shall be your judges. But if I cast out demons by the Spirit of God, then the kingdom of God has come upon you.
>
> "Or how can anyone enter the strong man's house and carry off his property, unless he first binds the strong man? And then he will plunder his house.
>
> "He who is not with Me is against Me; and he who does not gather with Me scatters.
>
> "Therefore I say to you, any sin and blasphemy shall be forgiven men, but blasphemy against the Spirit shall not be forgiven. And whoever shall speak a word against the Son of Man, it shall be forgiven him; but whoever shall speak against the Holy Spirit, it shall not be forgiven him, either in this age, or in the age to come (NASB).

The key verses, of course, are 31-32, "Therefore I say to you, any sin and blasphemy shall be forgiven men, but blasphemy against the Spirit shall not be forgiven. And whoever shall speak a word against the Son of Man, it shall be forgiven him; but whoever shall speak against the Holy Spirit, it shall not be forgiven him, either in this age, or in the age to come."

Blasphemy of the Holy Spirit is the term used to describe the unpardonable sin, yet it is not simple to understand. To blaspheme means to speak impiously. On the surface, one is tempted to think that you could say something impious about Jesus and be forgiven, but if you slipped and said something impious about the Holy Spirit, you were a goner. For example, Peter swore and denied that he ever knew Jesus, and that sin was forgiven. Yet, had he slipped and sworn and denied that he ever knew the Holy Spirit, would it have sealed his doom? I think not. There is more to it than that.

God will only reject us when we have ultimately rejected Him.

We must interpret any one passage in the Bible in light of all the other passages in the Bible. The Bible never contradicts itself. Therefore, we can sometimes gain insight into an unclear passage by looking at a clear passage. John 6:37 says, "The one who comes to Me I will by no means cast out." First John 5:12 says, "He who has the Son has life." Jesus makes it clear that if anyone comes to Him, He will not refuse him. He makes no exceptions. Jesus also makes it clear that if anyone has the Son, he also has eternal life. So a person's eternal destiny is linked to whether or not he believes in Jesus, repents, asks Jesus to forgive him, and commits his life to Him. If a person said something impious about the Holy Spirit and then came to Jesus, Jesus would not cast him out. So merely saying something impious about the Holy Spirit is not unpardonable.

The context of the passage must tell us what it means to "blaspheme the Holy Spirit." The Pharisees knew who Jesus was, had heard His message, and had rejected Him. Because they had rejected Him, they had to explain away the miracles He was performing. If they were not of God, then the Pharisees had only one other option. His work must have been of the devil. That is why they said that Jesus cast out demons by the power of the devil.

It is the Holy Spirit's task to convict people of their sin (John 16:8) and to illumine their minds to the truth of Scripture (1 Corinthians 2:12). Unless the Holy Spirit does these things, no one can come to Christ. The Holy Spirit had convicted the Pharisees of their sin and given them reason to believe in Jesus, but because of jealousy (Mark 15:10) the Pharisees rejected the Spirit's work in their heart. This clear, calculated rejection of the work of the Holy Spirit in their lives is unpardonable, because it demonstrates their rejection of God and Jesus. No one can go to heaven who rejects Jesus. As Jesus said in Matthew 12:37, "For by your words you will be justified, and by your words you will be condemned." Their words revealed their hearts, and as long as they rejected the work of the Holy Spirit who was trying to lead them to Jesus, that sin could not be pardoned.

James Packer, in his book *Concise Theology*, writes,

Such a sin would become unforgivable when the conscience had been so calloused by calling good evil that all sense of the moral glory of Jesus' mighty works was destroyed. This hardening of heart against Jesus would preclude any remorse at any stage for having thus blasphemed. But nonexistence of remorse makes repentance impossible, and nonexistence of repentance makes forgiveness impossible.

In the *Evangelical Dictionary of Theology*, we read,

In [Jesus], in his action, God was present and active in a decisive and final way—to reject his ministry was to reject God and so too forgiveness. The [unpardonable sin] is committed when a man recognizes the mission of Jesus by the Holy Spirit but defies and resists and curses it.

The consensus of opinion is that the unpardonable sin boils down to a rejection of Jesus, who was made known to us as God through the Holy Spirit's ministry to us. That squares with all the other passages in the New Testament that talk about salvation. So, as long as there is life, there is hope that someone will turn to Christ. And if one turns to Him, Jesus will certainly not cast him out. If you are concerned about it yourself, you have not yet committed the unpardonable sin. Simply turn to Jesus as the Scriptures instruct, and you will be born again (John 3:16), and the unpardonable sin will no longer be an issue for you.

SPEED BUMP!

Slow down to be sure you've gotten the main points of this section.

1. **Can we sin so often that God will not forgive us?**
We cannot sin so often that God will not forgive us.

2. **Can we sin so badly that God will not forgive us?**
We cannot sin so badly that God will not forgive us.

3. **What is the unpardonable sin?**
The unpardonable sin is rejecting the Holy Spirit's pull to bring us to Christ.

FOR FURTHER STUDY

Scripture Passages

- **Psalm 103:8-14**
- **Matthew 18:21-35**
- **Matthew 26:69-74**
- **Luke 23:34**

FAQ #35

What Does It Mean to Grieve the Holy Spirit?

We grieve the Holy Spirit when we choose, knowingly and willingly, to sin.

Central Passage: Ephesians 4:30, "Do not grieve the Holy Spirit of God, by whom you were sealed for the day of redemption."

Anyone with any age and experience has been grieved by the self-destructive behavior of loved ones. It drives an invisible knife into our hearts to see them make foolish or carnal or self-destructive decisions. It may be a daughter who marries a man who is not worthy of her, or a son who is hooked on alcohol or cocaine. Perhaps a brother, sister, or friend loses a good job because of dishonesty. Their behavior brings us inner pain.

In the same way, we can grieve the Holy Spirit. The Holy Spirit instructs us (1 John 2:27), illumines our minds to the truth of Scripture (1 Corinthians 2:12-13), convicts us of sin (John 16:8), and leads us in righteousness (Romans 8:14). It is the Holy Spirit who lives within us and tries to get us to live lives of holy service to God. When we disobey His instruction to us, it grieves Him. When He illumines our mind to the truth of a Scripture and we fail to obey, it grieves Him. When He convicts us of sin and tries to get us to turn from

"When Christians meet...to take counsel together, their purpose is not—or should not be—to ascertain what is the mind of the majority, but what is the mind of the Holy Spirit—something which may be quite different."

Margaret Thatcher
(former Prime Minister
of Great Britain)

sin, and we resist and rebuff Him, it grieves Him. It hurts Him much as it hurts us when someone we love wallows in self-destructive behavior. Our first step in responding to the Holy Spirit is to avoid grieving Him—to not disobey Him when He convicts us of sin.

FAQ #36

 **What Does It Mean to Quench the Holy Spirit?**

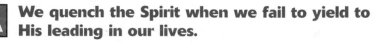 **We quench the Spirit when we fail to yield to His leading in our lives.**

Central Passage: **1 Thessalonians 5:19, Do not quench the Spirit.**

To quench means to stifle or extinguish. First Thessalonians 5:19 commands us, "Do not quench the Spirit." Of course, we cannot extinguish the Holy Spirit as a divine being, but we can extinguish His work in our lives by refusing to respond to or cooperate with His work in our lives. Philippians 2:12-13 says, "Work out your own salvation with fear and trembling; for it is God who works in you both to will and to do for His good pleasure."

Why Do I Need to Know This?

I need to know how to respond to the Holy Spirit so I will avoid the trap of living as though He had no role to play in my life. I would become a functional agnostic, living as though truth did not even exist. I would have diminished power to live as I ought, and diminished satisfaction with my life as a Christian and my relationship with God, to say nothing of the fact that my life would not be pleasing to Him.

The Holy Spirit, in addition to convicting us of sin, also supernaturally helps us understand the Bible, leads us, and guides us. The Holy Spirit places a thought or urging or conviction or sense of "ought-ness" in our minds to do something good and right. When we respond in faith and obedience to this work of God, then we are strengthened, spiritually enlarged, enlightened, and increased in our capacity to respond to something even greater next time. That is honoring the Holy Spirit. When we ignore His leading, or procrastinate, or make excuses, or simply disobey, that quenches the Holy Spirit. In addition, we are weakened, spiritually diminished, darkened in our understanding, and decreased in our capacity to respond to something even greater next time. That is dishonoring the Holy Spirit. The second step in responding to the Holy Spirit is to not quench Him—to not fail to yield our lives to His leading.

FAQ #37

 Q **What Does It Mean to Walk in the Spirit?**

 A **We walk in the Spirit when we consciously and prayerfully focus on the potential of the Holy Spirit's convicting, illuminating, leading, or enabling ministry coming to us at any moment, and keep ourselves prepared to follow and obey.**

Central Passage: **Galatians 5:16, Walk in the Spirit, and you shall not fulfill the lust of the flesh.**

There is no common agreement in Christendom as to what it means to walk in the Spirit, except on some very broad parameters. Therefore, I will try to stick within those parameters.

To walk in the Spirit must surely include something very close to trusting and obeying Christ, for the demands and the results are the same. We find that we are promised joy and peace through the Holy

Spirit ("Now may the God of hope fill you with all joy and peace in believing, that you may abound in hope by the power of the Holy Spirit," Romans 15:13), and yet the same things are promised to us through Jesus ("These things I have spoken to you, that My joy may remain in you, and that your joy may be full," John 15:11; "Peace I leave with you, My peace I give to you; not as the world gives do I give to you. Let not your heart be troubled, neither let it be afraid," John 14:27).

The purpose of the Holy Spirit is to glorify Christ.

Walking in the Spirit can also be seen as distinct from, though not divorced from, trusting and obeying Christ. To understand the Holy Spirit's ministry, and what we must do to walk in the Spirit, we must remember that the purpose of the Spirit's ministry is to glorify Christ. On the night of His betrayal Jesus said of the Spirit that "He will glorify me," and that the purpose of the Spirit's ministry is to "take of what is Mine [Jesus'] and declare it to you" (John 16:14). In other words, the Holy Spirit will cause Jesus to be glorious in people's eyes.

No understanding of the Holy Spirit is complete without understanding that the Father's purpose is that the Son be known, loved, honored, praised, worshiped, and made preeminent in everything, and that the Spirit's role is to make sure that happens. To focus on the Spirit in a way that causes us to overlook Christ is a mistake that contradicts the basic work of the Spirit.

Step 1: Repenting of Sin

The will of God for us is our sanctification, our being set apart for His fellowship and His service. That means that the first step in walking in the Spirit is consciously and prayerfully focusing on the Holy Spirit's convicting ministry in our lives, living in a state of preparedness to repent. As the Holy Spirit convicts us of sin in our lives (makes our sin known to us), we must repent, or turn around. Since we are imperfect and immature beings, repentance could be defined as "turning from as much as you know of your sin to give as much as you know of yourself to as much as you know of

God," and as your knowledge and maturity grow, your capacity to repent grows. Everything the Christian is and does must be seen in light of one overriding fact: He belongs to Christ and has been separated from everything and everyone in creation in order to belong to his God alone. Again, as Packer writes "Ordered, costly, unstinting commitment for the Lord's sake to spouse, children, parents, employers, employees, and all one's other neighbors, on the basis of being radically detached from them all to belong to God—Father, Son and Spirit—and to no one else, is the unvarying shape of the authentically holy life" (*Keep in Step with the Spirit*, p. 105).

Step 2: Responding to Truth

Our second step in walking in the Spirit is focusing on the potential of the Holy Spirit to illumine our minds to a truth of Scripture and living in a state of preparedness to follow and obey. The illuminating ministry of the Spirit is that supernatural work in which He enables us to understand the spiritual truths of the Scripture and their application to our lives (1 Corinthians 2:11-16). It may be in a quiet time of personal devotion or in the hubbub of life that the Scripture comes alive to us. We understand it, or we understand how it applies to us in a given situation. We see the truth, the way. It now remains for us to walk in the truth we now understand. When we do, we are walking in the Spirit, for the Spirit enabled us to understand the truth of Scripture. When we don't, we are grieving the Holy Spirit; for we know what we should do and we don't do it. That is sin (Romans 14:23).

Step 3: Following His Leading

The third element of walking in the Spirit is consciously and prayerfully focusing on the potential of the Holy Spirit's leading in our lives and keeping ourselves prepared to follow. This is a little more tricky, because we must discern whether or not something is the "leading of the Lord" before we are obligated to follow it. We do this by searching the Scripture, prayer, counsel from friends, assessment of circumstances, and so forth. However, to be frank, sometimes the leading of the Lord comes in quick, seemingly insignificant spurs of the moment, to do something good for someone. My pastor in seminary used to say, "Follow your good impulses. It is probably the Holy

Spirit." I always took that as good advice. You don't have to make a pro and con list and meditate on it for twenty-four hours if the impulse comes to you to say something encouraging and kind to someone. Often the Spirit ministers through us powerfully when we obey such impulses. If the matter is something transparently good, and must be done right away or the opportunity will be lost, you are pretty safe to go ahead and do it. The bigger things, of course, require more attention.

Step 4: Doing His Work

The fourth element of walking in the Spirit is consciously and prayerfully focusing on the potential for the Holy Spirit's enabling ministry to come to us at any moment and keeping ourselves prepared to follow and obey. This is very similar to the Spirit's leading, but often we may fear we are not able to do something we think God may be asking of us. Of course, God will never ask anything of us that we cannot do, but prudence sometimes demands that we think something through before jumping off the high dive. On the other hand, the Holy Spirit may have clearly gifted us for a certain ministry and we need to be ready to minister, knowing that He has enabled us. Or, He may choose to use us in a totally new way, so we must be ready to consider that possibility and obey if it becomes evident that God is leading us.

THINKING BACK

So many of us long for power—power to withstand the trials of life, or power to be effective in service to God. We long for power to bring meaning to our lives, to reassure us that we matter to God and that He is, in fact, using us. We long for power to overcome the sin and the habits and the weaknesses that drag us down in our pursuit of a meaningful relationship with the Lord. In the pursuit of these legitimate longings, we often look to satisfy them through quick fixes rather than a consistent commitment to Jesus and His holiness.

When you look up "power" in an English Bible concordance, you will find that occurrences of "power" after the Book of Acts usually do not refer to things we would ordinarily call miraculous. They more commonly link with the subtle but powerful things of the deeper inner life. For example, we see God's power revealed in the life of individual Christians in ways that we usually think of as common, everyday. Yet if the Bible is true, the common and everyday in the Christian life are also miraculous and powerful. And, when you think of such "mere" Christian living done consistently, we see it more clearly for what it is: true, spiritual power.

SPEED BUMP!

Slow down to be sure you've gotten the main points of this section.

1. **What does it mean to grieve the Holy Spirit?**
We grieve the Holy Spirit when we choose, knowingly and willingly, to sin.

2. **What does it mean to quench the Holy Spirit?**
We quench the Spirit when we fail to yield to His leading in our lives.

3. **What does it mean to walk in the Spirit?**
We walk in the Spirit when we consciously and prayerfully focus on the potential of the Holy Spirit's convicting, illuminating, leading, or enabling ministry coming to us at any moment, and keep ourselves prepared to follow and obey.

FOR FURTHER STUDY

Scripture Passages

- John 16:8
- Romans 8:14
- 1 Corinthians 2:11-16
- Galatians 5:16-23

- Ephesians 4:30
- 1 Thessalonians 5:19
- 1 John 2:27

FAQ #38

 What Is the Fruit of the Spirit?

 The fruit of the Spirit are character qualities that God possesses and that the Holy Spirit imparts to us as we live in trusting obedience to Jesus.

The description of the fruit of the Spirit has a very logical place in the argument of the Book of Galatians. The apostle Paul is arguing that there are two ways to live the Christian life. One is by obeying a long set of dos and don'ts. The other is by walking by the Spirit. Paul is saying that these believers should not resort to rule-keeping—even if the rules are the great Law of Moses. Instead, they should respond to the leading and direction of the Holy Spirit. Whenever people do, they begin to experience the fruit of the Holy Spirit. When they don't, they experience the fruit of the flesh.

The law puts the believer into bondage. The Spirit gives the believer freedom. Paul's appeal is to "Stand fast therefore in the liberty by which Christ has made us free, and do not be entangled again with a yoke of bondage" (Galatians 5:1).

The fruit of the Spirit, then, is our focus and goal. When we read over that marvelous list, who would not want those qualities to characterize his life? Who doesn't want peace, love, and joy? Who doesn't want to be patient, kind, and good? It would take a hard heart to turn that down. But often we don't want to pay the price to gain them. Too often, we want to

> "I've never known a person whom I thought was truly filled with the Holy Spirit who went out and bragged about it or sought to draw attention to himself."
>
> *Billy Graham*

"sow to the flesh" and reap the Spirit. It doesn't work.

Nine qualities embody the fruit of the Spirit, and in Billy Graham's book *The Holy Spirit*, he observes that these nine fruit are divided into three clusters of three.

Love, joy, and peace make up the first cluster. They especially speak of our Godward relationship. The second "cluster"—patience, kindness and goodness—especially is seen in our manward relationship, that is, our relationship with other people. The third "cluster" of faithfulness, gentleness and self-control is especially seen in our inward relationship—the attitudes and actions of the inner self.

At the same time, of course, these three "clusters" are all related to each other, and all should characterize our lives. And all will characterize our lives when we abide in Christ and allow the Holy Spirit to do His work in us (p. 187).

Why Do I Need to Know This?

If I don't know that the fruit of the Spirit are character qualities that God wants me to possess, I may miss out on the spiritual growth and personal transformation God intends for me. Unless I realize that they are the fruit of the Spirit rather than mere self-effort, I might become unduly frustrated when my self-effort does not produce the results I want to see in my life. I must know about the fruit and cooperate with God in the process of acquiring the fruit, but rely and trust in Him for the appearance of the fruit in my life.

This statement not only helps break down the subject for more in-depth study, but it also makes it easier to memorize the fruit of the Spirit.

FAQ #39

 What Is Love?

 Love is the steady direction of our will toward the lasting good of another.

I consider *Ben Hur* one of the greatest stories ever written. General Lew Wallace was an unbelieving Civil War general who, after the war, decided to write a book to discredit Christianity. After intense personal study, he became a Christian; and instead of writing a book to discredit Christianity, wrote one to reveal to the world who Christ really was, the Son of God.

The story is also a story of profound human love. Judah Ben Hur was a young, wealthy nobleman in Jerusalem, falsely accused of trying to kill the new Roman governor. Without trial, he was sent as a slave to row in the belly of a military ship. No one ever survived the slave ships. His mother and sister were arrested and sent to prison, which was little better than a slave ship. Few survived for long in those dark, dank, rat-infested, disease-ridden tombs for the living.

All seemed hopeless, yet one thought possessed Judah, drove him, and forced him to live: somehow he had to get home to Jerusalem to free his mother and sister from prison.

Opportunity began to unfold when his ship was damaged in a battle and began sinking; Judah saved the commander of the fleet from drowning. As a reward, he was taken to Rome and given his freedom. From there he made his way to Jerusalem, only to learn that his mother and sister had contracted leprosy in prison and were now existing as "living dead" in a leper colony outside the city. The most feared disease of the ancient world had turned them into monsters, with disfigured faces, and stumps where their hands and feet should have been. Because it was a contagious disease, all lepers were required to live apart from the rest of society.

Throwing aside concern for his own well-being, Judah went to the leper colony and, in a tender and moving gesture, took his mother and sister in his arms and removed them from the colony. This was the moral equivalent of taking on himself the disease that was mutilating his loved ones, since he knew he could easily contract the disease from them. At the urging of a friend, he took them to Jesus, but unfortunately, just in time to see Him crucified. They thought all hope was lost; but as the sky turned dark, lightning flashed, thunder rolled, and earthquakes shook, Judah's mother and sister were cleansed of their leprosy through faith in Jesus.

Love gives of itself for another.

Now, I haven't forgotten that this is fiction. This story did not happen, but it still contains a great truth. Judah's love for his mother and sister compelled him to give of what he had for the need of another. No price was too great to save his loved ones if he could.

We cannot, of course, love everyone with that degree of sacrifice. We can only be in one place at a time. But this story shows us a little of what love is. Love gives of itself for the needs of another.

First Corinthians 13:4-7 describes the kind of love God wants to guide our lives:

Love is patient, love is kind, and is not jealous; love does not brag and is not arrogant, does not act unbecomingly; it does not seek its own, is not provoked, does not take into account a wrong suffered, does not rejoice in unrighteousness, but rejoices with the truth; bears all things, believes all things, hopes all things, endures all things (NASB).

This, of course, is the kind of love He demonstrated toward us. In spite of my sin, when all of my sins were in the future, Christ died for my sins. He went to the cross so that I would not have to suffer eternal separation from God. Romans 5:8 says that God demonstrated His love toward us, in that, "while we were still sinners, Christ died for us."

God calls us to Christlike love.

Christ knew the worst about us, but He still died and then held out His hand to us and said, "Come to me, and I will give you eternal life." That kind of love is difficult to fathom, yet it is the kind of love that God calls us to live out. He promised us that kind of capacity when He said that the fruit of the Spirit is love. We can have that kind of love.

In fact, love is to be the mark of a Christian. The apostle John recorded Jesus' words, "By this all will know that you are My disciples, if you have love for one another" (John 13:35). Again, John wrote, "We know that we have passed from death to life, because we love the brethren [fellow Christians]" (1 John 3:14). The apostle Paul wrote, "Owe nothing to anyone except to love one another; for he who loves his neighbor has fulfilled the law" (Romans 13:8 NASB).

No matter what else we might say or do, if we do not have love, our life is a failure. Love is greater than any other characteristic, word, or deed. Again, the apostle Paul wrote, "If I speak with the tongues of men and of angels, but do not have love, I have become a noisy gong or a clanging cymbal. And if I have the gift of prophecy, and know all mysteries and all knowledge; and if I have all faith, so as to remove mountains, but do not have love, I am nothing. And if I give all my possessions to feed the poor, and if I deliver my body to be burned, but do not have love, it profits me nothing" (1 Corinthians 13:1-3 NASB).

God's love acts—it gives.

Francis Schaeffer, an evangelical theologian, has even gone so far as to say that love was the "badge" of a Christian. Not only does the apostle John say that if we love one another, we demonstrate to the world that we are Christ's disciples, but also that this love would produce unity. In John 17:21, Jesus prayed to the Father that "they [Christians] all may be one, as You, Father, are in Me, and I in You; that they also may be one in Us, that the world may believe that You sent Me."

Therefore, Schaeffer reasoned, if the world does not see us loving one another and living in unity, then the world has reason to believe that we are not Christ's disciples, and that Jesus was not sent from God. Interestingly enough, in a survey a number of years ago the two most important reasons non-Christians gave for not being Christians were (1) all the hypocrites in the church, and (2) they didn't believe that Jesus was God. Interesting correlation!

This helps us grasp the phenomenal importance of living in love. It is no accident, I think, that love is mentioned first in the fruit of the Spirit. Paul wrote in 1 Corinthians 13:13, "Now abide faith, hope, love, these three; but the greatest of these is love."

C. S. Lewis wrote a small book enti- **Love is** tled *The Four Loves* that may help us understand the kind of love that is a **the Christian's badge** fruit of the Spirit. Lewis was a brilliant scholar in literature who taught at Oxford **of identity.** and Cambridge universities. He was also a devout Christian and applied his profound intellect to helping make Christianity more understandable. There are four words in Greek, the original language of the New Testament, that are all translated into English as "love." They are *eros*, meaning physical love; *philos*, meaning the love of friendship; *storge*, meaning family love; and *agape*, meaning divine love.

When the Bible describes God's love for us, and the love that He wants and even commands us to have, the word used is *agape* (pronounced uh-gop'-ay). This word was virtually unknown in the ancient world, because it was so foreign to human behavior. When Matthew recorded the words of Jesus when He said, "Love your enemies," he used *agape*. When John recorded Jesus' words to love one another, he used agape. When Mark recorded Jesus' words, "You shall love your neighbor," he used *agape*.

Today, love is usually understood to be an emotion or feeling. There can be emotion associated with *agape*, but it is much more than that, as we see from the descriptions of the word in the Bible.

"Love," said Bishop Neill, "is the steady direction of the will toward another's lasting good" (*The Christian Character*, p. 22). *Agape* love acts, does, gives. When the Bible said, "For God so loved the world that He gave His only begotten Son" (John 3:16), it did not mean that goose pimples ran up and down God's spine when He looked at humanity. Rather, it meant that God was prepared to direct His will toward our lasting good.

FAQ #40

 What Is Joy?

 Joy is a deep sense of well-being that is not dependent upon favorable circumstances, but rooted in a fundamental acceptance of, and confidence in, the will of God.

I mentioned Corrie ten Boom earlier who was imprisoned in a Nazi concentration camp for helping Jews escape Nazi persecution. The suffering she experienced was beyond description, and she told her story in the remarkable book, *The Hiding Place*. After she was providentially released from the concentration camp, she traveled all over the world with the message that the light of Jesus is greater than the darkness of any sin. Her post-concentration camp story is told in a number of different books, including *Tramp for the Lord*. In this latter book, she told of going to a prison in Rwanda, Africa, which was one of the worst she had ever seen. Prisoners lived in squalor, sat in steaming mud in the open air, and wore masks of despair, hopelessness, and anger.

"What could I, an old Dutch woman, say to these miserable men that would help their lives?" I wondered.

"Lord," I prayed, "I am not able to overcome this darkness."

"Take My promise of Galatians 5:22," I heard an inner voice say.

Quickly I took my Bible and opened it to that passage. "But the fruit of the Spirit is love."

"Thank you, Lord," I whispered. "But I have a great love for these men already or I would not be here."

I read on. "But the fruit of the Spirit is love, joy."

"Joy?" I asked. "In these surroundings?" Then I remembered what Nehemiah said, "The joy of the Lord is my strength."

"Yes, Lord," I cried out. "That is what I need. That is what I claim. I claim the promise of joy."

I began to talk of the joy that is ours when we know Jesus. What a Friend we have in Him. He is always with us. When we are depressed, He gives us joy. When we do wrong, He gives us the strength to be good. When we hate, He fills us with His forgiveness. When we are afraid, He causes us to love.

Several faces changed and I saw that some of my joy was spilling over on them. But I knew what the rest were thinking: *After your talk you can go home, away from this muddy, stinking prison. It is easy to talk about joy when you are free. But we must stay here.*

Then she told them her story of the hardship, deprivation and suffering she experienced in the concentration camp. The hunger, the dehumanization, the lack of sleep, standing in line for hours outside as the icy-cold wind ripped through them, the lack of medical attention, the disease. One morning during roll call a woman collapsed.

In a moment a young woman guard was standing over her, a whip in her hand, screaming in rage, "Get up. How dare you think you can lie down when everyone else is standing?"

I looked out at the men who were sitting in front of me. No longer were their faces filled with darkness and anger. They were listening—intently—for they were hearing from someone who had walked where they were now walking.

"Say, men," I said, "do you know Jesus is willing to live in your hearts? He says 'I stand at the door of your heart and knock. If anyone hears my voice and opens the door, I come in.' Just think: that same Jesus loves you and will live in your heart and give you joy in the midst of all this mud. He who is willing, raise his hand."

Joy comes as a by-product.

I looked around. All the men, including the guards, had raised their hands. It was unbelievable, but their faces showed a joy that only the Holy Spirit could produce.

A missionary turned to her as they drove away later.

"I must confess to you that I thought this place was too dark for the light of the Gospel. I had been here once before and was so frightened I said I would never come back. Now... I have seen what the Holy Spirit can do. The joy of the Lord is available, even for such a place as this. From now on I shall return every week to tell them about Jesus."

Months later I received a letter from her in which she said, "The fear is gone. The joy remains" (*Tramp for the Lord*, pp. 81-82).

Joy is an illusive thing. The world knows almost nothing about it. They have settled for the "pursuit of happiness," which has come to mean the acquisition of people, possessions, and favorable circumstances. And since whatever affects the world also affects the church, Christians in America are stunted in their capacity for joy.

Joy is not so easily obtained, however, as momentary happiness might be. Joy is deeper.

Joy is not dependent on favorable circumstances, but on a proper outlook on life.

You may be euphoric if you win $10 million in a publisher's sweepstakes. You may be ecstatic if you receive a job promotion. You may be thrilled when you drive your new car off the lot. But none of these things will give you lasting joy—only momentary happiness.

Joy does not come by pursuing joy. Joy comes as a by-product of pursuing God and the good of others. Since American society elevates self above others, it knows very little about true joy.

I have been captain of a victorious athletic team, out in the middle of a basketball floor, receiving a trophy for winning a tournament, with hundreds of screaming fans voicing their delirious approval. That was one of the happiest experiences of my life, but there was no joy. Joy is knowing that God will somehow get me through whatever trial I face, and that in the end, all will be well.

I also have been at the bedside of someone dying of Lou Gehrig's disease. She had lost control of bodily movement and was quickly losing the ability to talk or swallow. In just a few days, she would have to be fed artificially and eventually put on a respirator. We both knew she would die a terrible death quite soon. We talked about Jesus, and death, and heaven. It was one of the unhappiest moments of my life, but there was deep joy.

Happiness and joy don't always go together.

If we live for the same things the world lives for (people, possessions, and favorable circumstances), then instead of experiencing joy, we will experience constant frustration. We will be frustrated over not being able to control things completely enough or long enough for our life to be consistently "happy," and frustrated with God for not blessing our lives and answering our selfish prayers. Furthermore, if we were able to get enough control (or enough luck) to get life going our way consistently, life would soon become meaningless. We were not created to live for ourselves; we were created to live for God and for others. We will never know joy any other way.

FAQ #41

 What Is Peace?

 Peace is the absence of anxiety and the presence of trusting assurance in the promises of God.

The third fruit of the Spirit, peace, is a gift that the Holy Spirit gives us when we believe the promises of God. Most Christians would say that they believe the promises of God. When we feel turmoil in our lives, however, it is often because of a promise in Scripture that we do not know about, do not understand, or do not believe. In Matthew 6:19-34 we are promised that God will feed and clothe us. Then it exhorts us to "not worry about tomorrow, for tomorrow will worry about its own things. Sufficient for the day is its own trouble" (v. 34). Yet I do find myself agitated and in turmoil over tomorrow. I fear that God will not be true to His word. When I see a problem that appears to have no solution, I often get anxious rather than resting in the fact that God knows the solution.

The Lord ministered to me deeply during one difficult time in my life as I read the account of the parting of the Red Sea in Exodus 14. The Israelites had left Egypt and were camped on the west bank of the Red Sea. The sea was to the east of them, mountains to the north and south, and then, here came the Egyptian army bearing down on them from the west. On three sides they were hemmed in, and now catastrophe was pressing down on them on the fourth side, with no solution in sight. God told Moses to stand still and see the salvation of the Lord. Then God parted the Red Sea, allowing the Israelites an escape route.

Often in our lives there is no solution to our problems on the horizon, but God lives beyond the horizon and can bring solutions we cannot foresee. We must remember that God has promised to see

God has solutions we cannot see.

us through the trials of this life. If we trust His promises, we can have peace in the midst of difficult circumstances. God has assured us that in this life all things work together for good to those who love Him, and that no temptation will overtake us but that He will provide a way of escape that we might be able to bear it. The Scriptures are laden with promises that, as we have the grace to believe, will build peace into the core of our being.

This does not mean that life will always be easy. On the contrary, life is often filled with physical pain, emotional turmoil, spiritual upheaval. So we must understand peace not as an elimination of troubling circum- stances, but as an assurance and trust in God in spite of our circumstances. In the midst of fighting the trials of life you might sometimes hear me say, "I am okay at the core. I'm just a little frayed around the edges." Life certainly will "fray" us around the edges, but at the core, as we grow in the grace and knowledge of our Lord Jesus Christ, the fruit of the Spirit increasingly can be ours.

God does not ask more than we can give.

THINKING BACK

The fruit of the Spirit is just that. It is not the fruit merely of self-effort, though some self-effort is required of the Christian before he will experience the fruit. But self-effort alone will not produce the fruit of the Spirit.

Remember the experience I described earlier of when as a young Christian I became exceedingly frus- trated at the lack of progress in my spiritual life? I had doubled my efforts in prayer, Scripture study, memorization, and reading, as well as my witnessing and service to God; but my intensified efforts produced nothing. I felt that God wanted me to be more spiritual than I was, but no matter how hard I tried, I could not seem to speed up my growth.

The breakthrough began for me when I heard a seminary professor say, "You can't be holy in a hurry." No one had ever told me before that God was willing to put up with my immaturities, much as a parent is willing to put up with a two-year-old's immaturities. The parent certainly looks forward to the day when the two-year-old will grow out of the "terrible twos," but until that time the parent will not expect more than reasonable progress.

As I look back at that experience more than twenty-five years later, I see I was, like any child, impatient to be more mature. However, my desire was frustrated by the assumption that God expected me to be more mature than I was. When I understood that God was not asking more of me than I could give, I was able to be satisfied and dissatisfied with my spiritual life at the same time. I was dissatisfied in that I wanted to be more mature and knew that God eventually expected me to be more mature. But I could be satisfied in the sense that, if the fruit of the Spirit did not come purely by my own effort, and if my present stage of spiritual growth was all the Holy Spirit had given me, I had to be content with the work of God in my life. It is always God's perfect will that we be like Jesus, but it is within His permissive will that He gives us time to grow into His likeness.

SPEED BUMP!

Slow down to be sure you've gotten the main points of this section.

1. What is the fruit of the Spirit?

The fruit of the Spirit are character qualities that God possesses and that the Holy Spirit imparts to us as we live in trusting obedience to Jesus.

2. What is love?

Love is the steady direction of our will toward the lasting good of another.

3. What is joy?

Joy is a deep sense of well-being that is not dependent upon favorable circumstances, but rooted in a fundamental acceptance of, and confidence in, the will of God.

4. What is peace?

Peace is the absence of anxiety and the presence of trusting assurance in the promises of God.

FOR FURTHER STUDY

Scripture Passages

Several passages speak of the fruit of the Spirit, and of love, joy, and peace. Study them further to see how they add to your understanding of these issues.

- John 14:1-3, 27
- John 15:1-11
- 1 Corinthians 13:4-7
- Galatians 5:22-23

FAQ #42

 What Is Patience?

 Patience is the ability to endure unpleasant people or circumstances for a higher cause.

I heard of a man who decided to get away from the

> "Lord, teach me to silence my own heart that I may listen to the gentle movement of the Holy Spirit within me and sense the depths which are of God."
>
> *Elijah de Vidas*
> *(Sixteenth Century)*

rat race of the corporate world, so he joined a monastery that required a vow of silence. Just the thing, he thought, for reducing the frustration and upheaval of his former life. In the monastery, he was allowed to say two words every five years.

After the first five years, he was called into his superior's office, who asked, "Do you have anything you would like to say? You have two words."

The man said, "Bad food!"

He returned to his life at the monastery, and after another five years he was again given the opportunity to say two words.

"Hard bed!" he said, and returned once more to his normal life at the monastery.

Five years passed again, and again he was before his superior, who asked him if he had two words he would like to say.

The man said, "I quit!"

His superior said, "Well, I'm not surprised. You've done nothing but complain since you got here!"

Patience is relative, I suppose. His "superior" thought he had done nothing but complain since he arrived, but I thought he exercised some pretty amazing patience. He endured bad food and a hard bed for fifteen years with only four words of complaint.

Patience (or "long suffering" in the King James Version), the fruit of the Spirit, comes from a Greek word that means to remain steadfast under provocation. It means "hanging in there" when you feel like you are merely hanging. It carries the thought of patiently enduring

Why Do I Need to Know This?

1. I need to know this so I will have a complete view of the maturity level God wants me to have.

2. I need to know this so I will not excuse weaknesses in my character.

3. I need to know this so I will trust God to make me mature and not think I can do it on my own.

bad treatment without retaliation or revenge. If we are irritable, vengeful, resentful, or malicious in our relationships with others, we are "short-suffering," not "long-suffering."

It is a difficult virtue to get and keep, as you well know if you have ever been treated unjustly or accused of something falsely by someone you thought was your friend. Patience can prove elusive if you have been passed up for a promotion, or failed to get a job, with the position going to someone whom you believed to be your inferior. A spouse who treats you badly or ignores you requires enormous patience, as does someone who tells a hurtful truth about you in an unkind way.

We also need patience in the face of other problems: illness or injury that takes a long time to heal, or never heals; financial problems you are powerless to overcome; loved ones who are self-destructing through drugs, alcohol, sex, or crime; or underachievement in your vocation or home.

Patience is a virtue that the Holy Spirit will build into our lives as we live in trusting obedience to Him. The apostle Paul wrote that we can be "strengthened with all might, according to His glorious power, for all patience and longsuffering with joy" (Colossians 1:11). Patience comes from the power of God when we rely on Him, refusing to give in to our natural inclinations to lash out or withdraw—to give in to anger or despair. Even when the current of events is flowing against us, we must swim up the emotional stream of life and allow the Holy Spirit to empower us with patience.

FAQ #43

 What Is Kindness?

 Kindness is treating others well in word and deed.

Abraham Joshua Heschel, a Jewish rabbi, used to say, "When I was young, I admired clever people. Now that I am old, I admire kind people." (Harold Kushner, *When All You've Ever Wanted Isn't Enough*, p. 58). I'm with Rabbi Heschel. The older I get, the more I admire kind people. Kindness is one of the greatest virtues and most admired, even while it is one of the rarest. How many acts of kindness have you witnessed lately? How many acts of kindness have you done lately? We admire kindness when we see it, and we appreciate it when we experience it, but we often shy away from acts of kindness ourselves. Kindness often costs us something, and we fear becoming a victim, unsure whether we are actually performing an act of kindness or getting taken in by someone.

I remember several years ago seeing a woman standing beside a busy street in the cold with a sign in her hand, "Need money to get home. Willing to work." I drove past her, as did thousands of other people, and just as I had with many other people before. But this time it was different. The Holy Spirit got a headlock on me and wouldn't let me go. I couldn't forget that young woman. It was Thanksgiving weekend and very cold out. Her nose was running, her eyes were red, her hands were chapped. I thought, "If this lady is trying to find an 'easy way out' in life, she miscalculated. What she is doing is harder than working."

I talked to her, and she said she was trying to get home and ran out of money. She couldn't get a job, because all the likely places to get a job (fast-food restaurants, etc.) required that she have a phone number, and she didn't have one. She was staying at a rescue mission, so she wasn't starving to death, but she was between a rock and a hard place. To this day, I don't know if her problem was legitimate or not, but I gave her enough money for a bus ticket home, which was not an insignificant amount of money. She might have bought cocaine with the money for all I know. However, the issue right then was not between her and me. It was between God and me. He wanted to know if I cared enough about people to risk getting taken in.

I am not suggesting that everyone ought to give money to people like that. All I know is that God used that moment to test me. Who owned the money in my bank account? Who prioritized the time it took me to talk to her and then go to the bank and get the money? I performed an act of kindness that day, but I almost shied away because I wasn't sure I wanted to pay the price.

A thousand other opportunities for acts of kindness can be missed for the same reason, but on a smaller scale. My wife and I used to live in a neighborhood in which a lot of minority students would come by selling candy and "nicknacks" we didn't need. Initially I responded by just nicely getting rid of them. But I didn't feel good about it. They were, I became persuaded, doing the best thing they knew to earn a little money. I had sold door-to-door before and knew it wasn't easy. I began to admire their "grit." So I changed my strategy. Instead of getting rid of them, I began asking the kids how much profit they made on their monster candy bar. Then, instead of buying the candy bar, I would give them the amount of profit they would have made if I had bought the candy (I didn't want to eat the thing). If they were selling worthless things, I would often buy them anyway, just to be kind and encourage them in their enterprise. Proverbs 19:17 says, "He who is gracious to a poor man lends to the LORD, and He will repay him for his good deed" (NASB).

> **G**od **wants to know if we care enough to pay the price.**

By giving these examples, I am not suggesting that everyone follow my example. I am not even saying that I would do the same thing again in every instance. I am just saying that we must be alert to opportunities to be kind to others and respond when the Lord prompts us.

We also can be kind to those in spiritual or emotional need. I once read, "We should always be kind to others, for they may be walking life's road wounded." How that struck me. I had walked wounded many times, and I was profoundly grateful when others were kind to me.

I will never forget something that happened when I was in seminary. Those were difficult times. Seminary was extremely demanding academically. I had to work so much that I didn't have enough time to study, but I had to study so much that I couldn't work enough to make a decent living (I just heard a loud amen from fellow seminarians). Time and money were too short for many friends or recreation. I was pretty discouraged.

One morning I pulled into the seminary parking lot for my first class, and the professor pulled in at the same time. He got out of his car, turned to wait for me, greeted me, and chatted amiably as he walked me into the classroom. As long as I live I will never forget that simple act of kindness. He was not even conscious of having done anything, but it fed me deeply, spiritually and emotionally. Memory of that simple incident has spurred me to be alert for opportunities to be kind.

Be **alert for those who are walking life's road wounded.**

I try especially to be kind to people at checkout counters and other such places where people often aren't kind to them. I try to have a pleasant word to say. I believe that if we cultivate the habit of kindness in small things, we will also be even more ready to be kind in bigger things.

I fail many times when I am preoccupied or hurting a little myself. We all do. But be kind to others. You may be lending to the Lord, and the person you are kind to may be walking life's road wounded. Think how grateful you would be in their shoes. Use discretion, but be sensitive. Be ready to be kind whenever you think Jesus would be kind.

FAQ #44

 What Is Goodness?

 Goodness is doing that which is beneficial for others.

Goodness and kindness are so similar that it is often hard to distinguish between the two. I don't know if it is a valid distinction, but I often think of kindness as being very personal, face to face, whereas goodness need not always be as personal. Someone might give a sum of money to help build a hospital. That gesture, to me, seems more good than kind, because it is an indirect benefit to people rather than a direct benefit. The benefactor might not even give the money to an individual but to a nonprofit corporation. People you don't even know and never see, months and years later, reap the benefits.

I once read a story about ricocheting goodness:

V. P. Menon was a significant political figure in India during its struggle for independence from Britain after World War II. He was the highest-ranking Indian in the government, and it was to him that Lord Mountbatten turned for the final drafting of the charter plan for independence.

Eldest son of twelve children, he quit school at thirteen and worked as a laborer, coal miner, factory hand, merchant, and schoolteacher. He talked his way into a job as a clerk in the Indian administration, and his rise was meteoric—largely because of his integrity and brilliant skills in working with both Indian and British officials in a productive way. Both Nehru and Mountbatten mentioned his name with highest praise as one who made practical freedom possible for his country.

He had a reputation for personal charity which began when Menon arrived in Delhi to seek a job in government, and all his possessions, including his money and I.D., were stolen at the railroad station. In desperation he turned to an elderly Sikh, explained his troubles, and asked for a temporary loan of fifteen rupees to tide him over until he could get a job. The Sikh gave him the money. When Menon asked for his address so that he could repay the man, the Sikh said that Menon owed the debt to any stranger who came to him in need, as long as he lived. The help came from a stranger and was to be repaid to a stranger.

Menon never forgot that debt—neither the gift of trust nor the fifteen rupees. He was generous to the needy the rest of his life.

This story was told to me by a man whose name I do not know. He was standing beside me in the Bombay airport at the left-baggage counter. I had come to reclaim my bags and had no Indian currency left. The agent would not take a traveler's check, and I was uncertain about getting my luggage and making my plane. The man paid my claim-check fee—about eighty cents—and told me the story as a way of refusing my attempt to figure out how to repay him. His father had been Menon's assistant and had learned Menon's charitable ways and passed them on to his son. The son had continued the tradition of seeing himself in debt to strangers, whenever, however. (Excerpted from Robert Fulghum, *All I Really Need to Know I Learned in Kindergarten*, pp. 154-155.)

That's good—very good. We all ought to try to do more good than we do. Everyone wins.

FAQ #45

 What Is Faithfulness?

 Faithfulness is being reliable in doing what you should do.

Clarence Jordan was a man of unusual abilities and commitment. He had two Ph.D.s, one in agriculture and one in Greek and Hebrew. He could have chosen to do anything he wanted. He chose to serve the poor. In the 1940s, he founded Koinonia Farm in Americus, Georgia. It was a community for poor whites and poor blacks— an idea that did not go over well in the Deep South of the '40s.

Ironically, much of the resistance came from good church people who were as committed to the laws of segregation as the other folk in town. For fourteen years the town people tried everything to stop Clarence. They tried boycotting him, and slashing workers' tires when they came to town, with no effect.

Finally, in 1954, the Ku Klux Klan had enough of Clarence Jordan, so they decided to get rid of him once and for all. They came one night with guns and torches and set fire to every building on Koinonia Farm but Clarence's home, which they riddled with bullets. And they chased off all the families except one black family which refused to leave.

Clarence recognized the voices of many of the Klansmen, and some of them were church people. Another was the local newspaper's reporter. The next day, the reporter came out to see what remained of the farm. The rubble still smoldered and the land was scorched, but he found Clarence in the field, hoeing and planting.

> **W**e are not about success but faithfulness.

"I heard the awful news," he called to Clarence, "and I came out to do a story on the tragedy of your farm closing."

Clarence just kept on hoeing and planting. The reporter kept prodding, trying to get a rise from this quietly determined man who seemed to be planting instead of packing his bags. Finally, the reporter said in a haughty voice, "Well, Dr. Jordan, you got two of them Ph.D.s and you've put fourteen years into this farm, and there's nothing left of it at all. Just how successful do you think you've been?"

Clarence stopped hoeing, turned toward the reporter with his penetrating blue eyes, and said quietly but firmly, "About as successful as the cross. Sir, I don't think you understand us. What we are about is not success but faithfulness. We're staying. Good day." Beginning that day, Clarence and his companions rebuilt Koinonia, and the farm is going strong today. (Excerpted from Tim Hansel, *Holy Sweat*, pp. 188-189.)

Faithfulness is being trustworthy; it is "hanging in there"; it is persevering. It is being the kind of person who can be counted on to do what is right. Over and over in the Bible, we are admonished to be faithful. Matthew 25:21 says that if we are faithful in little things, the Lord will give us bigger things. In Revelation 2:10 we read, "Be faithful until death, and I will give you the crown of life."

We should be faithful to our word. We should be faithful to our responsibilities. But above all we should be faithful to God. God wants to be able to count on us. If we let Him, the Holy Spirit will help make us faithful people. Do you have a weakness in being faithful? Many do. It is not a highly valued characteristic in modern America. But it is highly valued to God.

FAQ #46

 What Is Gentleness?

 Gentleness is treating others carefully, with respect and sensitivity.

A parable is told about the sun and the wind arguing which one was more powerful. The sun quietly asserted that he was the strongest, while the wind protested loudly.

"See that traveler walking along the road down there?" the wind asked. "Whichever of us makes him take his coat off first is the most powerful." The sun agreed.

The wind blew short, violent bursts to rip the coat off the traveler, but the man only clutched the coat closer to himself. The wind escalated to great, furious gales, but to no avail. The traveler simply wrapped his coat about him as tightly as possible and leaned into the punishing wind.

Finally, the wind was exhausted and could blow no longer. Then the sun came out and began shining soft, gentle light upon the traveler. After a while, a little bead of perspiration began to roll down the traveler's forehead. Before long, the coat came off, as the traveler succumbed to the sun's gentle warmth.

In human relationships, gentleness is like the sun, and aggression is like the wind. One disarms while the other antagonizes.

Gentleness is being easy on others, taking into account their vulnerable points, and taking care not to hurt them. I recently had some dental work done in a clinic where more than one dentist worked on me. One dentist had rough hands; the other had gentle hands. The first dentist hurt me; the second one didn't. That is part of what it means to be gentle.

The biblical word translated "gentle" goes beyond this limited meaning of the word. It is sometimes translated "meek." One who is meek is often understood to be timid, weak, and "wimpy." Such is not the case, however. The Greek word carries with it the idea of "power under control." Until he was matured by the Holy Spirit, the apostle Peter was loud and pushy. Then, he became controlled and channeled, using his great energy for the glory of God. Moses is mentioned in the Bible as the "meekest" man who ever lived. Yet he was far from a wimp. He was a dramatic and powerful leader, but under the control of God. A river that is controlled can generate much power. A fire under control can warm a house. A personality under control can be used by God for His purposes. Controlled energy can achieve great good. Uncontrolled energy usually just destroys.

Jesus was arrested, taken through a series of mock trials, beaten, and mistreated. He had the power to annihilate his tormentors with a spoken word, but He didn't, choosing instead to endure suffering for the sake of our redemption. Isaiah spoke prophetically when he said of Jesus, "He was oppressed and He was afflicted, yet He opened not His mouth; He was led as a lamb to the slaughter, and as a sheep before its shearers is silent, so He opened not His mouth" (Isaiah 53:7). Meekness is "love under control."

The Holy Spirit will build gentleness within us. When He does, we do not hurt people or run roughshod over them. We do not "lock horns" with those who cross us. Rather, under the control of the Holy Spirit, we display sensitivity to others and allow God to channel our energy for the good of others.

Goodness is love under discipline.

FAQ #47

 What Is Self-control?

 Self-control is the ability to resist immediate gratification for the sake of a higher goal.

Someone once said, "I can resist everything except temptation." That's the way it is with most of us. I have found that I can do whatever I want to do—except make myself want to do the right thing *all* the time. The Holy Spirit, however, cannot be tempted, and He does want to do the right thing all the time. So, what we lack in self-control, the Holy Spirit can supply.

A person without self-control is like a ship at full sail in a strong wind with no rudder. People without self-discipline miss deadlines, are always late, eat too much, get too angry too often, drink too much, become too sexually involved, are too lazy, watch too much TV, speak too often without concern for others, fail to perform up to their potential, act dishonestly, etc., etc., etc. Lack of self-control is a life-wasting, life-destroying thing.

Living without control can waste your life.

By nature and natural habit I am not a self-disciplined person. Yet I discovered in my college years that I would never get the things I wanted in life unless I paid the price. That required self-discipline. There are people who say to me now, "I am amazed at how disciplined you are." To that, I can only respond, "That is the Holy Spirit." He is the one who gave me the insight and conviction that I needed self-discipline, and then He built His discipline in me.

Self-control is one of the most difficult character qualities to possess, because we don't want to do the things we should. If we wanted to do them, it wouldn't take self-control. Yet, it is also one of the greatest character qualities to possess. Solomon said, "He who is slow to anger is better than the mighty, and he who rules his spirit than he who takes a city" (Proverbs 16:32).

What is your area of greatest weakness? The Holy Spirit wants to give you self-control in this area. However, we often have to mature or grow into self-control, which obviously takes time. In the meantime, we can help protect ourselves by getting others to help us. It might be our pastor, or members of a Bible study or other small group, or someone who will agree to disciple us. We in America are so independent that we think we can and should do everything alone. But God did not intend for Christians to strive alone. He intended us to be so involved in one another's lives that we would strengthen one another and help one another do the things we ought to do and not do the things we ought not to do. And, of course, we can pray for one another that the Holy Spirit will give us the self-control we need to live lives that honor Him.

THINKING BACK

In conclusion, I want to make four observations.

1. *I doubt if the list of the fruit of the Spirit is exhaustive.* The apostle Paul listed the works of the flesh in Galatians 5:19-21. Certainly, his list of sins was not exhaustive. Now, in the next two verses, he lists the fruit of the Spirit; and they, too, are probably not exhaustive. But they are representative. These kinds of character qualities are true of the Holy Spirit, and He wants them to be true of us. In time, He will give us even more.

2. *The fruit of the Spirit are a unit.* Paul calls them the fruit of the Spirit, not the fruits of the Spirit. That is, they are a "whole" and when you get one of the list, you are on your way to them all. For example, a person would not be "loving" if he were not also "kind." He would not be "good" if

he were not also "gentle." I like the idea that these are not
nine "fruits" but nine facets of one fruit.

Certainly, because of temperament, upbringing, culture, and background, some of the fruit may come more easily to a person than others. For example, one might find kindness coming more quickly then self-control. However, the Holy Spirit brings spiritual maturity, and maturity covers all nine characteristics.

3. *These are the fruit of the Spirit, not the fruit of self-effort.*
We are to strive for obedience to Christ. We are not to be
passive in the pursuit of Christ's character. Yet even in our
best pursuit, we must be patient and wait for the Spirit to
build these qualities into our lives as a whole fruit.

4. *Just because love, joy, peace, etc. are fruit of the Spirit*
does not mean non-Christians cannot experience them, at
least in some measure. Many non-Christians are kind and
self-controlled. It isn't that all people who manifest these
character qualities are mature Christians, but that all mature
Christians will manifest these character qualities.

The bottom line is that these character qualities reflect the spirit and nature of God. As we mature and allow the Holy Spirit to rule our lives, God is glorified, our lives are enriched and satisfied, and the unsaved are given a favorable picture of God by what they see of Him in our lives.

SPEED BUMP!

Slow down to make sure you've gotten the main points of this section.

1. What is patience?
Patience is the ability to endure unpleasant people or circumstances for a higher cause.

2. What is kindness?

Kindness is treating others well in word and deed.

3. What is goodness?

Goodness is doing that which is beneficial for others.

4. What is faithfulness?

Faithfulness is being reliable in doing what you should do.

5. What is gentleness?

Gentleness is treating others carefully, with respect and sensitivity.

6. What is self-control?

Self-control is the ability to resist immediate gratification for the sake of a higher goal.

FOR FURTHER STUDY

Scripture Passages

- John 14:1-3, 27
- John 15:1-11
- 1 Corinthians 13:4-7
- Galatians 5:22-23

BIBLIOGRAPHY

Anders, Max E. *30 Days to Understanding the Bible*. Nashville: Thomas Nelson Publishers, 1998.

Anders, Max E. *30 Days to Understanding the Christian Life*. Nashville: Thomas Nelson Publishers, 1998.

Black, Carl. "All in a Day's Work," *Reader's Digest*. August 1993.

Brand, Paul, and Philip Yancey. *Fearfully and Wonderfully Made*. Grand Rapids: Zondervan, 1980.

Elwell, Walter (ed.). *Evangelical Dictionary of Theology*. Grand Rapids: Baker Book House Co., 1984.

Foss, Sam Walter. "The House by the Side of the Road." Quoted by William Bennett in *The Book of Virtues*. New York: Simon & Schuster, 1993.

Fulghum, Robert. *All I Really Need to Know I Learned in Kindergarten*. New York: Villard Books, 1988.

Graham, Billy. *The Holy Spirit*. Dallas: Word, Inc., 1988.

Green, Michael P. *Illustrations for Biblical Preaching*. Grand Rapids: Baker Book House Co., 1988.

Haggai, John. *Winning over Pain, Fear and Worry*. New York: Inspirational Press, 1991.

Hansel, Tim. *Holy Sweat*. Dallas: Word, Inc., 1987.

Kushner, Harold. *When All You've Ever Wanted Isn't Enough*. Thorndike, ME: Large Print Books, 1987.

Lewis, C. S. *The Four Loves*. San Diego, CA: Harvest Books, 1991.

Neill, Stephen. *The Christian Character*. New York: Association Press, 1955.

Packer, James I. *Concise Theology*. Wheaton, IL: Tyndale, 1993.

Packer, James I. *Keep in Step with the Spirit*. Grand Rapids: Fleming H. Revell, 1987.

Schaeffer, Francis. "The Mark of a Christian." Appendix to *The Church at the End of the 20th Century*. Downer's Grove, IL: InterVarsity Press, 1970.

Schaeffer, Francis. *True Spirituality*. Wheaton, IL: Tyndale, 1972.

Ten Boom, Corrie. *Tramp for the Lord*. Fort Washington, PA: Christian Literature Crusade, Inc., 1974.

Vine, W. E. *Vine's Complete Expository Dictionary of Old and New Testament Words*. Nashville: Thomas Nelson Publishers, Inc., 1996.

Wallace, Lew. *Ben Hur*. Provo, UT: Regal Publications, 1993.

Yancey, Philip. "Vital Issues." *Guidance*. Portland, OR: Multnomah Press, 1983.